AMiGURUMi AFFIRMATIONS

I only
have eyes
for you.
If you've got it,
haunt it!
You sprinkle
happiness wherever
you go.
Life's a fiesta—
celebrate
every bite!
You're out of
this world.
Need some
morel support?
Don't get your
feathers ruffled.
Don't let
the pressure
get to you.

AMIGURUMI AFFIRMATIONS

* 30 *

cute and easy crochet projects to brighten your day and lift your spirits

Lee Sartori

Quarto.com

First Published in 2026 by Quarry Books, an imprint of
The Quarto Group, 100 Cummings Center, Suite 265-D,
Beverly, MA 01915, USA.
T (978) 282-9590 F (978) 283-2742

EEA Representation, WTS Tax d.o.o.,
Žanova ulica 3, 4000 Kranj, Slovenia.
www.wts-tax.si

10 9 8 7 6 5 4 3 2 1

ISBN: 978-0-7603-9770-1

Digital edition published in 2026
eISBN: 978-0-7603-9771-8

Library of Congress Cataloging-in-Publication Data available

Design and Page Layout: Kelley Galbreath
Photography: Zack Bowen, LLC, except Glenn Scott Photography on pages 16–23 (stitch photos only) and Lee Sartori on page 144

Printed in Guangdong, China TT092025

For Sean,

who has yet to have a book dedicated to him. Mongo is appalled.

Acknowledgments

I would like to thank the teams at Lion Brand Yarn, WeCrochet, and Furls Crochet for their continued support of my work. Also, to my amazing editor, Michelle, the biggest thanks.

You're top dog!

Let's avo-cuddle.
Don't be afraid to color outside the lines.
Keep cool.
If you're dragon, I'll be there to pick you up.

CONTENTS

Introduction

Welcome to a world where yarn, creativity, and positivity intertwine in the most delightful way! In this book, we'll embark on a journey through the charming craft of crocheting amigurumi—tiny, crocheted treasures that bring smiles, warmth, and a touch of whimsy to any space. From cute animals to playful food items and beyond, these lovable little characters are more than just crochet projects—they hold a message. Each amigurumi you create will hold up its own little encouraging sign, offering a heartfelt sentiment that can brighten anyone's day.

In the fast-paced world we live in, we could all use a reminder of the little joys, and what better way to spread that positivity than with a handmade creation that's both adorable and uplifting? Whether you're gifting your amigurumi to a friend, placing it on your desk as a pick-me-up, or simply crocheting for the love of the craft, these projects will offer a unique way to share a little encouragement.

As you work your way through the pages, you'll find easy-to-follow patterns that will guide you in creating a

variety of fun and endearing characters. From a cheerful avocado reminding you that "You've guac this" to a lovable ghost holding up a "You have a boo-tiful spirit" sign, each project is designed to help you express love, optimism, and creativity through crochet.

Whether you're a seasoned crocheter or a beginner, this book offers something for everyone. So grab your hook, choose your favorite yarn, and let's begin crafting these adorable amigurumi creations that are sure to spread smiles wherever they go. Happy crocheting!

We have included printed cards with affirmations at the back of the book for you to cut out. You can also download those and more by scanning this QR code.

CHAPTER 1

GETTING STARTED

Before we start stitching, let's cover the essentials! This chapter will guide you through the basic crochet stitches and the supplies you'll need to create your adorable characters. Whether you're a beginner or refreshing your skills, we'll ensure you're fully equipped to begin crafting!

Helpful INFORMATION

Here is some useful information for following the patterns in this book, including the crochet abbreviations used in the patterns and conversions for US and UK crochet terms, and advice on getting the correct gauge.

Abbreviations

beg = begin(ning)
BLO = back loop(s) only
ch = chain(s)
dc = double crochet
FLO = front loop(s) only
hdc = half double crochet
inv-dec = invisible decrease
rep = repeat
rnd(s) = round(s)
RS = right side
sc = single crochet
sc2tog = single crochet 2 stitches together
sk = skip
sl st = slip stitch
sp(s) = space(s)
st(s) = stitch(es)
WS = wrong side

Term Conversions

Crochet techniques are the same universally, and everyone uses the same terms. However, US patterns and UK patterns are different because the terms denote different stitches. Here is a conversion chart to explain the differences.

US TERM	UK TERM
single crochet (sc)	double crochet (dc)
half-double crochet (hdc)	half treble (htr)
double crochet (dc)	treble (tr)
triple crochet (tr)	double treble (dtr)

MATERIALS: Everything You Need to Create Good Vibes

Creating amigurumi is a wonderfully creative process that begins with selecting the right materials. While there are endless options, choosing the best supplies will ensure that your finished projects are both beautiful and durable, with just the right amount of charm. Here's a guide to the key materials you'll need to bring your amigurumi to life.

The Yarn

Each of these little amigurumi is crocheted with medium-weight yarn in a variety of colors. The wonderful thing about them is that they make excellent stash busters! I used worsted weight yarns from Lion Brand Yarn, WeCrochet, and Furls Crochet to find the perfect colors, but if you don't have the exact same orange or red as shown in the book, that's okay! Just be sure to check that each of the yarns you choose have a similar texture, whether that be cotton, acrylic, or wool, and that they are all the same thickness. Use what you have and make each piece unique to you!

TIP **These little amigurumi don't use very much yarn. Check your stash to see if you already have what you need!**

The Crochet Hook

There are so many amazing crochet hooks out there to choose from! Whether you are using a crochet hook from Clover, WeCrochet, Furls Crochet, or Tulip, just be sure to use a hook that feels right to you and gives you the results you're looking for. While this book doesn't require an exact match for gauge to crochet your amigurumi, it is a great idea to check the label on your yarn choice to see what size crochet hook is recommended. Matching your hook to the yarn is the best way to get a lovely fabric

6.00mm

out of your crochet! For amigurumi, it's best to use the hook that gives you a dense fabric and doesn't allow any stuffing to show through.

The Safety Eyes

I used small, 6 mm safety eyes for the designs in this book, but you can opt for some fun changes! Use larger eyes, add felt to the back of the eyes, or even opt to use embroidered eyes instead! There are so many ways to change up the faces on these little cuties, like adding sleepy eyes, eyelashes, eyebrows, and more. I ordered my safety eyes on Amazon, but you can also find them on the WeCrochet website in lots of sizes and colors.

All the Little Extras

To complete your amigurumi affirmations, you'll need a few extra things like stitch markers, stuffing, craft wire, and paper. I used polyester fiberfill stuffing for my amigurumi, and the good news is you don't need much! For the arms, I used craft wire that you can find at any craft store in spools. The wire is perfect because it is lightweight, and you can bend it to change the direction of your amigurumi's arms and have them stay in place. The signs were printed on thick paper on my home printer. We have provided some ready-made signs at the back of the book as well as downloadable signs. Glue your signs to the hands, and you are all set!

CROCHET Stitches & Techniques

The patterns in this book use mostly very common crochet stitches and techniques that you're probably already familiar with. If you haven't used them before or need a refresher, check out the instructions and photos in this section.

Magic Loop

The magic loop technique is a method used to start projects in the round. It creates a tight, adjustable loop. Hold the yarn in your hand and form a loop, leaving a small tail **(Figs. 1 and 2)**. Insert your hook into the loop **(Fig. 3)** and yarn over to pull up a loop **(Fig. 4)**. Ch 1, then you can now work the required number of stitches into the loop. Once your stitches are in place, gently pull the yarn tail to tighten the loop and close the center.

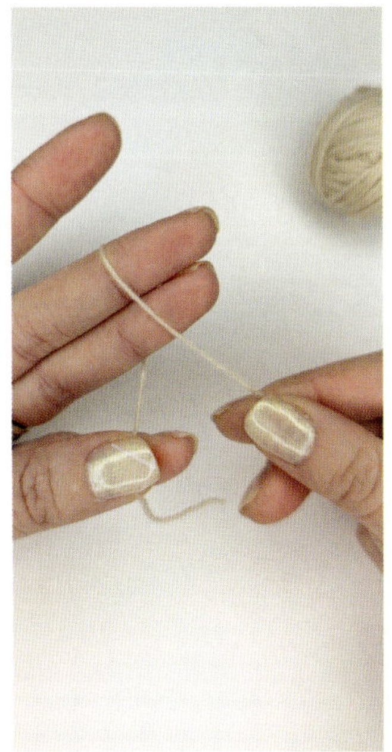

FIGURE 1

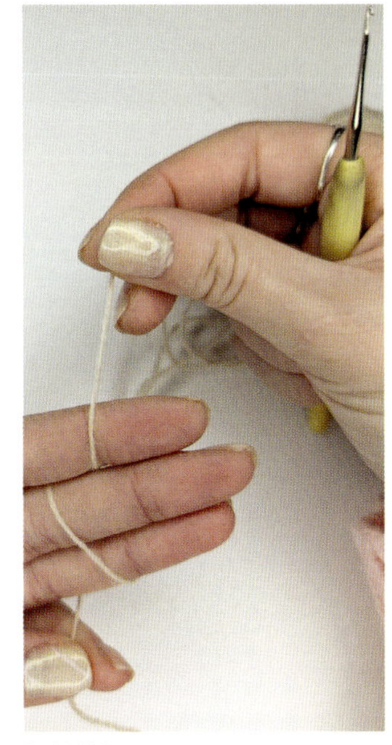

FIGURE 2

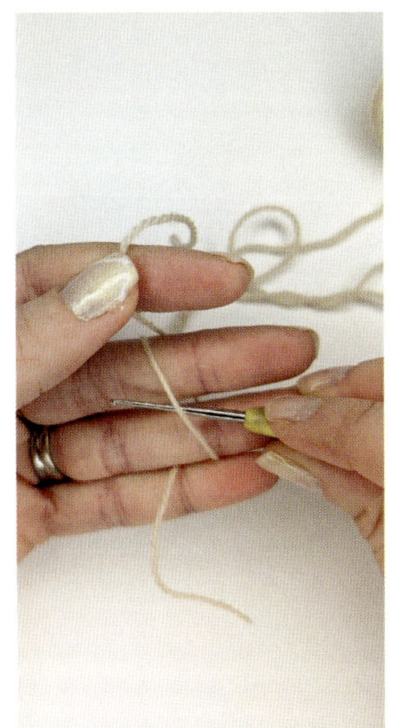

FIGURE 3

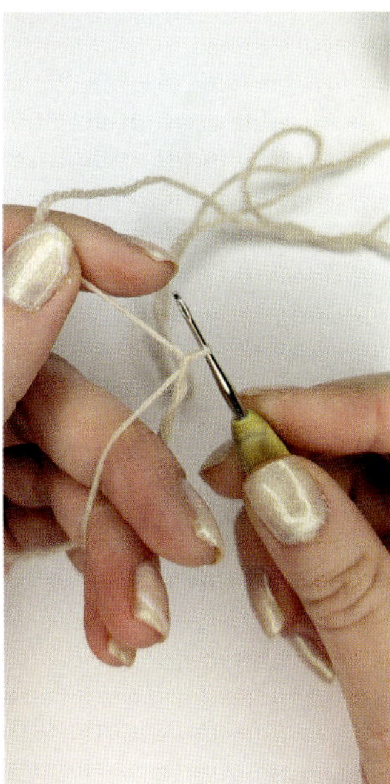

FIGURE 4

FIGURE 5

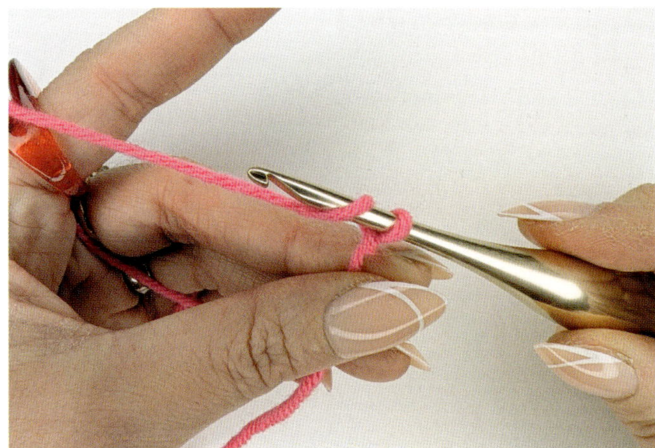

FIGURE 6

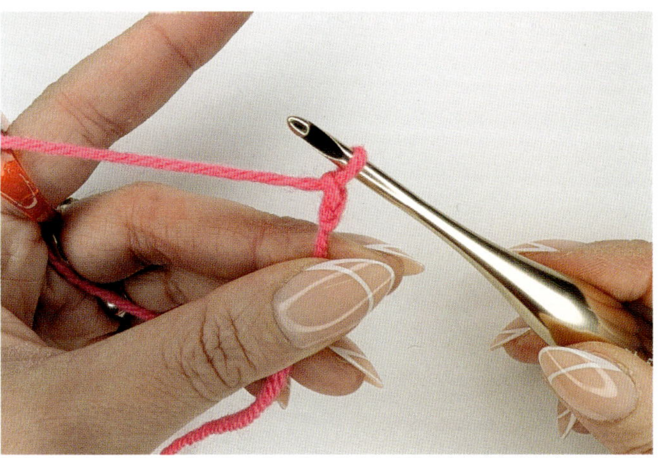

FIGURE 7

FIGURE 8

Chain (ch)

All crochet begins with a chain, into which you work the foundation row for your piece. To make a chain, start with a slip knot. To make a slip knot, make a loop several inches from the end of the yarn, insert the hook through the loop, and wrap the working yarn over the hook from back to front. Draw the yarn through the loop on the hook **(Fig. 5)**. After the slip knot, start your chain. Wrap the yarn from back to front over the hook (yarn over) and catch it with the hook **(Fig. 6)**. Draw the yarn through the loop on the hook **(Fig. 7)**. You have now made 1 chain. Repeat the process to make a row of chains **(Fig. 8)**. When counting chains, do not count the slip knot at the beginning or the loop that is on the hook.

Single Crochet (sc)

Insert the hook into the specified stitch **(Figs. 9 and 10)**, wrap the yarn over the hook, and draw the yarn through the stitch so there are 2 loops on the hook **(Figs. 11 and 12)**. Wrap the yarn over the hook again and draw the yarn through both loops **(Figs. 13 and 14)**. You should now have just one loop on your hook. When working in single crochet, always insert the hook through both top loops of the next stitch, unless the directions specify front loop or back loop only.

FIGURE 9

FIGURE 10

FIGURE 11

FIGURE 12

FIGURE 13

FIGURE 14

Completed row of single crochet stitches

Half Double Crochet (hdc)

Wrap the yarn over the hook **(Fig. 15)**, insert the hook into the specified stitch **(Fig. 16)**, and wrap the yarn over the hook again. Draw the yarn through the stitch so there are 3 loops on the hook **(Fig. 17)**. Wrap the yarn over the hook and draw it through all 3 loops at once **(Fig. 18)**. You should now have just one loop on your hook.

FIGURE 15

FIGURE 16

FIGURE 17

FIGURE 18

FIGURE 19

FIGURE 20

FIGURE 21

FIGURE 22

FIGURE 23

FIGURE 24

Double Crochet (dc)

Wrap the yarn over the hook **(Fig. 19)**, insert the hook into the specified stitch, and wrap the yarn over the hook again **(Fig. 20)**. Draw the yarn through the stitch so there are 3 loops on the hook **(Fig. 21)**. Wrap the yarn over the hook again and draw it through 2 of the loops so there are now 2 loops on the hook **(Fig. 22)**. Wrap the yarn over the hook again **(Fig. 23)** and draw it through the last 2 loops, ending with one loop on your hook **(Fig. 24)**.

FIGURE 25

FIGURE 26

FIGURE 27

FIGURE 28

FIGURE 29

Several slip stitches in a row

Skip (sk)

Sometimes a pattern will call for skipping over a certain number of stitches to create a gap. When you reach the stitch or chain you need to skip, simply pass over it without working into it. Do not insert your hook into the stitch or chain; just move on to the next stitch or chain as instructed in your pattern **(Figs. 25 and 26)**.

Slip Stitch (sl st)

Insert your crochet hook into the stitch (or space) where you want to work the slip stitch **(Fig. 27)**. Wrap the working yarn around your hook from back to front, just like you would for a regular stitch. Pull the yarn directly through the stitch **(Fig. 28)** and then through the loop already on your hook **(Fig. 29)**. You should now have just one loop on your hook.

Back Loop Only (BLO)

Insert the hook through the back loop only of each stitch, rather than under both loops of the stitch **(Fig. 30)**. Complete the stitch as usual **(Fig. 31)**.

FIGURE 30

FIGURE 31

Front Loop Only (FLO)

Insert the hook through the front loop only of each stitch, rather than under both loops of the stitch **(Fig. 32)**. Complete the stitch as usual **(Figs. 33 and 34)**.

FIGURE 32

FIGURE 33

FIGURE 34

FIGURE 35

FIGURE 36

FIGURE 37

FIGURE 38

FIGURE 39

Single Crochet 2 Together (sc2tog)

This decreases the number of stitches in a row or round by 1. Insert the hook into the specified stitch, wrap the yarn over the hook **(Fig. 35)**, and draw the yarn through the stitch so there are 2 loops on the hook **(Fig. 36)**. Insert the hook through the next stitch, wrap the yarn over the hook **(Fig. 37)**, and draw the yarn through the stitch so there are 3 loops on the hook **(Fig. 38)**. Wrap the yarn over the hook again and draw the yarn through all the loops at once **(Fig. 39)**. You should now have just one loop on your hook.

Invisible Decrease (inv-dec)

The invisible decrease is worked over the next two stitches you would normally decrease. Insert your hook into the front loop of the first stitch **(Fig. 40)**. Without pulling through, insert your hook into the front loop of the next stitch as well **(Fig. 41)**. Yarn over and pull through both front loops, just as you would with a regular single crochet. Now you have 2 loops on your hook **(Fig. 42)**. Yarn over again and pull through both loops to complete the decrease **(Fig. 43)**. You should now have just one loop on your hook.

FIGURE 40

FIGURE 41

FIGURE 42

FIGURE 43

I'll be frank.
You're the best.
I'll never
dessert you.
You and tacos
make everything
better.
Chill out, you're
crushing it!

Chapter 2

COMFORT FOOD

FOR THE SOUL

In this chapter we'll take a bite of the deliciously fun world of crocheted food! From a cheerful donut to a hot dog that's frankly adorable, these amigurumi treats are sure to bring smiles. With their playful personalities and uplifting messages, each project is a perfect blend of creativity and sweetness—ideal for gifting or decorating your space!

You're kind of
a big dill.

PICKLE

We love a great sense of humor! A little bit sweet, a little bit tangy—it's what makes you so funny! We know you can tell a dill-icious joke with the best of them, and this delightful pickle is a reminder that finding the laughter in situations is the flavor we can all use in life!

AFFIRMATIONS for THE PICKLE

You're kind of a big dill.

Keep gherkin it!

Positive Pickle

You make life dill-icious.

If you're in a pickle,
I'll help you out.

Measurements
1½" (3.8 cm) × 5" (12.7 cm)

Yarn
Worsted weight (#4 medium)

Shown here: Furls Crochet Wander Acrylic, 120 yd (109 m), 3½ oz (100 g), 100% acrylic: 1 ball Arbor

Hook
US Size G/6 (4 mm) crochet hook. Adjust hook size if necessary to work tightly.

Gauge
Exact gauge is not critical for this piece. Work tightly to ensure stuffing does not show through.

Notions
Yarn needle
Polyester stuffing
Black embroidery thread
Black craft wire
1 pair 6 mm black safety eyes
Scissors
Stitch marker
Card stock
Hot glue or double-sided tape

Special Stitch
Cluster (3-dc cluster) = [Yarn over, insert hook in indicated st, yarn over and draw up a loop, yarn over and draw through 2 loops on hook] 3 times, yarn over and draw through 4 remaining loops.

Ch 2.

Rnd 1: Work 6 sc in 2nd ch from hook; do not join, work in continuous rnds—6 sc.

Place a marker in last sc made to indicate end of rnd. Move marker up as each rnd is completed.

Rnd 2: Work 2 sc in each st around—12 sc.

Rnd 3: [2 sc in next st, sc in next st] around—18 sc.

Rnd 4: [2 sc in next st, sc in next 5 sts] around—21 sc.

Rnd 5: [Sc in next 3 sts, Cluster in next st, sc in next 3 sts] around.

Rnds 6–10: Sc in each st around.

Rnd 11: [Cluster in next st, sc in next 6 sts] around—21 sts.

Rnds 12–16: Sc in each st around.

Rnd 17: Sc in BLO of next 10 sts, sc in next 11 sts.

Rnds 18–21: Sc in each st around.

Rnd 22: Sc in FLO of 10 sts from Rnd 17, sk first 10 sts of Rnd 21, sc in last 11 sts of Rnd 21.

Rnds 23–34: Rep Rnds 5–16.

Add safety eyes between Rnds 28 and 29, about 2 sts from each side of Cluster. Stuff Pickle and continue stuffing as work progresses.

Rnd 35: [Inv-dec, sc in next 5 sts] around—18 sc.

Rnd 36: [Inv-dec, sc in next st] around—12 sc.

Rnd 37: Inv-dec around—6 sc.

Fasten off, leaving a long tail for sewing. Sew remaining 6 sts closed.

Finishing

Cut a piece of black craft wire about 3½ to 4 times as long as the width of the piece. Gently poke the wire through center of Pickle at arm level, leaving equal-length ends sticking out of sides for arms.

Using black embroidery thread, embroider a smile in a V shape below the eyes.

Write or print an inspirational message on card stock and cut to desired size. Use hot glue or double-sided tape to attach sign to hands.

Weave in ends.

DONUT

Life is so much sweeter with you in it! You're like the icing on a donut, sprinkling happiness wherever you go. While this yummy-looking crocheted pink donut may not be edible, it's calorie free and here to remind you that it's a great idea to enjoy the sweet side of life!

AFFIRMATIONS for THE DONUT

Donut give up!

You're the icing on my donut.

You sprinkle happiness wherever you go.

Enjoy the sweet side of life!

I'll never dessert you.

Measurements
3" (7.6 cm) × 3" (7.6 cm)

Yarn
Worsted weight (#4 medium)

Shown here: Lion Brand Basic Stitch Anti Pilling, 185 yd (170 m), 3½ oz (100 g), 100% acrylic: 1 ball 202-125AA Truffle (A)

WeCrochet Brava Worsted, 218 yd (200 m), 3½ oz (100 g), 100% acrylic: 1 skein 28423 Cotton Candy (B)

Hook
US Size G/6 (4 mm) crochet hook. Adjust hook size if necessary to work tightly.

Gauge
Exact gauge is not critical for this piece. Work tightly to ensure stuffing does not show through.

Notions
Yarn needle
Polyester stuffing
Yellow embroidery thread
Blue embroidery thread
Black embroidery thread
Black craft wire
1 pair 6 mm black safety eyes
Scissors
Stitch marker
Card stock
Hot glue or double-sided tape

Donut
give up!

Donut Back

With A, ch 18; join with a sl st in first ch to form a ring.

Rnd 1: Ch 1, sc in each ch around; join with sl st in first sc—18 sc.

Rnd 2: [Sc in next sc, 2 sc in next sc, sc in next sc] 6 times; do not join, work in continuous rnds—24 sc.

Place a marker in last sc made to indicate end of rnd. Move marker up as each rnd is completed.

Rnd 3: [2 sc in next st, sc in next 3 sts] around—30 sc.

Rnd 4: [Sc in next 2 sts, 2 sc in next st, sc in next 2 sts] around—36 sc.

Rnd 5: [2 sc in next st, sc in next 5 sts] around—42 sc.

Rnds 6–8: Sc in each st around.

Fasten off, leaving a long tail for sewing.

Donut Front

With B, work same as Donut Back.

Add safety eyes between Rnds 4 and 5, about 4 sts apart.

Fasten off, leaving a long tail for sewing.

Legs (Make 1)

With A, ch 20.

Fasten off and trim ends.

Finishing

Hold RS of Front and Back together (WS facing out), with foundation chains matching. Sew base of foundation chains together. Turn piece RS out. Sew last rnds of Front and Back together through BLO of Front, and FLO of Back, stuffing piece before completing the seam.

Cut a piece of black craft wire about 2½ to 3 times as long as the width of the piece. Gently poke the wire through center of piece at arm level, leaving equal-length ends sticking out of sides for arms.

Thread Legs through bottom of Donut, leaving equal-length ends of ch-20 hanging down for legs. With A, sew a few stitches to secure Legs.

Using black embroidery thread, embroider a smile in a V shape below the eyes. Using yellow and blue embroidery thread, embroider small lines for sprinkles on the Donut Front.

Write or print an inspirational message on card stock and cut to desired size. Use hot glue or double-sided tape to attach sign to hands.

Weave in ends.

TACO

This adorable taco celebrates the joy of enjoying life's little moments! Packed with colorful yarn ingredients, it's a reminder to embrace both the spicy and sweet sides of life. Whether you're working through challenges or savoring victories, this taco will inspire you to always stay bold and flavorful.

AFFIRMATIONS for THE TACO

Wow, look at you! Taco-bout incredible!

Life's a fiesta—celebrate every bite!

A taco is spicy and full of zest—just like you!

Wrap yourself in positivity!

You and tacos make everything better.

Measurements

4" (10.2 cm) × 2" (5.1 cm)

Yarn

Worsted weight (#4 medium)

Shown here: Lion Brand Vanna's Choice, 170 yd (156 m), 3½ oz (100 g), 100% acrylic: 1 ball each 860-158I Mustard (A), 860-113 Scarlet (B), and 860-172 Kelly Green (C)

Hook

US Size G/6 (4mm) crochet hook. Adjust hook size if necessary to work tightly.

Gauge

Exact gauge is not critical for this piece. Work tightly to ensure stuffing does not show through.

Notions

Yarn needle
Polyester stuffing
Black embroidery thread
Black craft wire
1 pair 6 mm black safety eyes
Scissors
Stitch marker
Card stock
Hot glue or double-sided tape

Special Stitch

Cluster (2-dc cluster) = [Yarn over, insert hook in indicated st, yarn over and draw up a loop, yarn over and draw through 2 loops on hook] 2 times, yarn over and draw through 3 remaining loops.

Wow, look at
you! Taco-bout
incredible!

Taco Shell

With A, ch 2.

Rnd 1: Work 6 sc in 2nd ch from hook; do not join, work in continuous rnds—6 sc.

Place a marker in last sc made to indicate end of rnd. Move marker up as each rnd is completed.

Rnd 2: Work 2 sc in each st around—12 sc.

Rnd 3: [2 sc in next st, sc in next st] around—18 sc.

Rnd 4: [Sc in next st, 2 sc in next st, sc in next st] around—24 sc.

Rnd 5: [2 sc in next st, sc in next 3 sts] around—30 sc.

Rnd 6: [Sc in next 2 sts, 2 sc in next st, sc in next 2 sts] around—36 sc.

Rnd 7: [2 sc in next st, sc in next 5 sts] around—42 sc.

Rnd 8: [Sc in next 3 sts, 2 sc in next st, sc in next 3 sts]—48 sc.

Rnd 9: [2 sc in next st, sc in next 7 sts] around—54 sc.

Rnd 10: Working in FLO, [sc in next 4 sts, 2 sc in next st, sc in next 4 sts] around—60 sc.

Fasten off, leaving a long tail for sewing. Add safety eyes between Rnds 5 and 6, about 3 sts apart.

Toppings

With B, ch 10.

Row 1: Sc in 2nd ch from hook, [ch 1, sk next ch, sc in next ch] across— 5 sc and 4 ch-1 sps.

Fasten off B. With RS facing (do not turn), join C in first st of Row 1.

Row 2: With C, [Cluster in next ch-1 space, ch 1] across to last sc, sl st in last sc—4 Clusters.

Fasten off, leaving a long tail for sewing. Sew top of Row 2 to base of foundation ch.

Legs (Make 1)

With A, ch 20.

Fasten off and trim ends.

Finishing

Fold Taco Shell in half. Sew curved edges together by sewing through BLO of Rnd 9 sts, leaving edges of Rnd 10 open and stuffing piece before completing the seam.

Sew Toppings to center top edge of Taco, between edges of Rnd 10.

Cut a piece of black craft wire about 2½ to 3 times as long as the width of the piece. Gently poke the wire through center of piece just below toppings, leaving equal-length ends sticking out of sides for arms.

Thread Legs through bottom of Taco, leaving equal-length ends of ch-20 hanging down for legs. With a length of yarn, sew a few stitches to secure Legs.

Using black embroidery thread, embroider a smile in a V shape below the eyes.

Write or print an inspirational message on card stock and cut to desired size. Use hot glue or double-sided tape to attach sign to hands.

Weave in ends.

Positive
Potato

POTATO

You say "po-tay-to," I say "po-tah-to," but no matter how you say it, this potato is adorable! Unbothered and super "a-peeling," this charming spud is ready to sit in your corner and cheer you on!

AFFIRMATIONS for THE POTATO

Positive Potato

I only have eyes for you.

I find you so a-peeling.

I may be just a tiny potato, but I believe in you!

You're my best spud.

Measurements
3" (7.6 cm) × 2½" (6.4 cm)

Yarn
Worsted weight (#4 medium)

Shown here: Lion Brand Basic Stitch Anti Pilling, 185 yd (170 m), 3½ oz (100 g), 100% acrylic: 1 ball 202-125AA Truffle

Hook
US Size G/6 (4 mm) crochet hook. Adjust hook size if necessary to work tightly.

Gauge
Exact gauge is not critical for this piece. Work tightly to ensure stuffing does not show through.

Notions
Yarn needle
Polyester stuffing
Black embroidery thread
Black craft wire
1 pair 6 mm black safety eyes
Scissors
Stitch marker
Card stock
Hot glue or double-sided tape

Body

Ch 2.

Rnd 1: Work 6 sc in 2nd ch from hook; do not join, work in continuous rnds—6 sc.

Place marker in last sc made to indicate end of rnd. Move marker up as each rnd is completed.

Rnd 2: Work 2 sc in each st around—12 sc.

Rnd 3: [2 sc in next st, sc in next st] around—18 sc.

Rnd 4: [Sc in next st, 2 sc in next st, sc in next st] around—24 sc.

Rnds 5 and 6: Sc in each st around.

Rnd 7: [2 sc in next st, sc in next 7 sts] around—27 sc.

Rnd 8: [Sc in next 4 sts, 2 sc in next st, sc in next 4 sts] around—30 sc.

Rnd 9: [2 sc in next st, sc in next 9 sts] around—33 sc.

Rnd 10: [Sc in next 5 sts, 2 sc in next st, sc in next 5 sts] around—36 sc.

Rnd 11: [2 sc in next st, sc in next 11 sts] around—39 sc.

Rnd 12: [Sc in next 6 sts, 2 sc in next st, sc in next 6 sts] around—42 sc.

Add safety eyes between Rnds 8 and 9, about 3 sts apart.

Stuff Body and continue stuffing as work progresses.

Rnds 13–16: Sc in each st around.

Rnd 17: [Inv-dec, sc in next 5 sts] around—36 sc.

Rnd 18: [Sc in next 2 sts, inv-dec, sc in next 2 sts] around—30 sc.

Rnd 19: [Inv-dec, sc in next 3 sts] around—24 sc.

Rnd 20: [Sc in next st, inv-dec, sc in next st] around—18 sc.

Rnd 21: [Inv-dec, sc in next st] around—12 sc.

Rnd 22: Inv-dec around—6 sc.

Fasten off, leaving a long tail for sewing. Sew remaining 6 sts closed.

Legs (Make 1)

Ch 20.

Fasten off and trim ends.

Finishing

Cut a piece of black craft wire about 2½ to 3 times as long as the width of the piece. Gently poke the wire through center of piece at arm level, leaving equal-length ends sticking out of sides for arms.

Thread Legs through bottom of Potato, leaving equal-length ends of ch-20 hanging down for legs. With a length of yarn, sew a few stitches to secure Legs.

Using black embroidery thread, embroider a smile in a V shape below the eyes.

Write or print an inspirational message on card stock and cut to desired size. Use hot glue or double-sided tape to attach sign to hands.

Weave in ends.

AVOCADO

This little avocado is the toast of the town! If you're feeling down in the pits, just remember that it wants only what's good for you.

AFFIRMATIONS for THE AVOCADO

You've guac this!

Let's guac and roll.

Without you, life would be the pits.

Let's avo-cuddle.

Measurements
3½" (8.9 cm) × 3" (7.6 cm)

Yarn
Worsted weight (#4 medium)

Shown here: Furls Crochet Wander Acrylic, 120 yd (109 m), 3½ oz (100 g), 100% acrylic: 1 ball Patina (A)

Lion Brand Basic Stitch Anti Pilling, 185 yd (170 m), 3½ oz (100 g), 100% acrylic: 1 ball each 202-125AA Truffle (B), and 202-130B Grass (C)

Hook
US Size G/6 (4 mm) crochet hook. Adjust hook size if necessary to work tightly.

Gauge
Exact gauge is not critical for this piece. Work tightly to ensure stuffing does not show through.

Notions
Yarn needle
Polyester stuffing
Black embroidery thread
Black craft wire
1 pair 6 mm black safety eyes
Pink blush
Scissors
Stitch marker
Card stock
Hot glue or double-sided tape

You've guac this!

Body

With A, ch 2.

Rnd 1: Work 6 sc in 2nd ch from hook; do not join, work in continuous rnds—6 sc.

Place a marker in last sc made to indicate end of rnd. Move marker up as each rnd is completed.

Rnd 2: Work 2 sc in each st around—12 sc.

Rnd 3: [2 sc in next st, sc in next 3 sts] around—15 sc.

Rnd 4: [Sc in next 2 sts, 2 sc in next st, sc in next 2 sts] around—18 sc.

Rnd 5: [2 sc in next st, sc in next 5 sts] around—21 sc.

Rnd 6: [Sc in next 3 sts, 2 sc in next st, sc in next 3 sts] around—24 sc.

Rnd 7: Sc in each st around.

Rnd 8: [2 sc in next st, sc in next 3 sts] around—30 sc.

Rnd 9: [Sc in next 2 sts, 2 sc in next st, sc in next 2 sts] around—36 sc.

Rnd 10: [2 sc in next st, sc in next 5 sts] around—42 sc.

Rnds 11–17: Sc in each st around.

Rnd 18: [Inv-dec, sc in next 5 sts] around—36 sc.

Rnd 19: [Sc in next 2 sts, inv-dec, sc in next 2 sts] around—30 sc.

Rnd 20: [Inv-dec, sc in next 3 sts] around—24 sc.

Add safety eyes between Rnds 10 and 11, about 6 sts apart. Stuff Body and continue stuffing as work progresses.

Rnd 21: [Sc in next st, inv-dec, sc in next st] around—18 sc.

Rnd 22: [Inv-dec, sc in next st] around—12 sc.

Rnd 23: Inv-dec around—6 sc.

Fasten off, leaving a long tail for sewing. Sew remaining 6 sts closed.

Pit

With B, ch 2.

Rnd 1: Work 6 sc in 2nd ch from hook; do not join, work in continuous rnds—6 sc.

Place a marker in last sc made to indicate end of rnd. Move marker up as each rnd is completed.

Rnd 2: Work 2 sc in each st around—12 sc.

Rnd 3: Sc in each st around.

Fasten off, leaving a long tail for sewing.

Rind

With C, ch 2.

Rnd 1: Work 6 sc in 2nd ch from hook; do not join, work in continuous rnds—6 sc.

Place a marker in last sc made to indicate end of rnd. Move marker up as each rnd is completed.

Rnd 2: Work 2 sc in each st around—12 sc.

Rnd 3: [2 sc in next st, sc in next st] around—18 sc.

Rnd 4: [Sc in next st, 2 sc in next st, sc in next st] around—24 sc.

Rnd 5: Sc in next st, ch 5, sc in 2nd ch from hook and in next 3 ch, sc in same st, sc in next 3 sts, [2 sc in next st, sc in next 3 sts] 5 times—34 sc.

Rnd 6: Sc in next st, sc in underside of next 4 ch, 4 sc in 5th ch, sc in next 33 sts—42 sc.

Rnd 7: [Sc in next 3 sts, 2 sc in next st, sc in next 3 sts] around—48 sc.

Rnd 8: [2 sc in next st, sc in next 7 sts] around—54 sc.

Rnds 9–11: Sc in each st around.

Fasten off, leaving a long tail for sewing.

Finishing

Sew Pit to Body, between Rnds 13 and 18, adding a small amount of stuffing to shape the Pit as you sew.

Put Body inside Rind and sew Rind in place.

Cut a piece of black craft wire about 2½ to 3 times as long as the width of the piece. Gently poke the wire through center of Body at arm level, leaving equal-length ends sticking out of sides for arms.

Using black embroidery thread, embroider a smile in a V shape below the eyes.

Add a small amount of blush under each eye.

Write or print an inspirational message on card stock and cut to desired size. Use hot glue or double-sided tape to attach sign to hands.

Weave in ends.

You're one
smart cookie!

COOKiE

No matter which way your day crumbles, this cookie has your back. Some days are just crummy, but it's always good to remember that you'll find sweet moments sprinkled in like little chocolate chips.

AFFIRMATIONS for THE COOKIE

You're one smart cookie!

You've got the recipe for success.

I like you: You're sweet and a little bit nutty.

You're on a roll!

Measurements
3" (7.6 cm) × 3" (7.6 cm)

Yarn
Worsted weight (#4 medium)

Shown here: Lion Brand Basic Stitch Anti Pilling, 185 yd (170 m), 3½ oz (100 g), 100% acrylic: 1 ball each 202-121L Almond (A) and 202-125AA Truffle (B).

Hook
US Size G/6 (4 mm) crochet hook. Adjust hook size if necessary to work tightly.

Gauge
Exact gauge is not critical for this piece. Work tightly to ensure stuffing does not show through.

Notions
Yarn needle
Polyester stuffing
Black embroidery thread
Black craft wire
1 pair 6 mm black safety eyes
Scissors
Stitch marker
Card stock
Hot glue or double-sided tape

Cookie (Make 2)

With A, ch 2.

Rnd 1: Work 6 sc in 2nd ch from hook; do not join. Work in continuous rnds—6 sc.

Place marker in last sc made to indicate end of rnd. Move marker up as each rnd is completed.

Rnd 2: Work 2 sc in each st around—12 sc.

Rnd 3: [2 sc in next st, sc in next st] around—18 sc.

Rnd 4: [Sc in next st, 2 sc in next st, sc in next st] around—24 sc.

Rnd 5: [2 sc in next st, sc in next 3 sts] around—30 sc.

Rnd 6: [Sc in next 2 sts, 2 sc in next st, sc in next 2 sts] around—36 sc.

Rnd 7: [2 sc in next st, sc in next 5 sts] around—42 sc.

Fasten off.

Legs (Make 1)

With B, ch 20.

Fasten off and trim ends.

Finishing

Add safety eyes to one Cookie (for front), between Rnds 3 and 4 and in line with center of Cookie.

Using black embroidery thread, embroider a smile in a V shape between the eyes.

Using a length of B held double, embroider chocolate chips, randomly placed, over both front and back Cookies.

Place front and back Cookies together with sts matching and chocolate chips facing outward

Join Cookies: Working through both thicknesses, draw up a loop of A anywhere in edge of Cookies, ch 1, sc in each st around, stuffing Cookie lightly before completing seam; join with sl st in first sc. Fasten off.

Cut a piece of black craft wire about 3 to 3½ times as long as the width of the piece. Gently poke the wire through center of piece at arm level, leaving equal-length ends sticking out of sides for arms.

Thread Legs through bottom of Cookie, leaving equal-length ends of ch-20 hanging down for legs. With a length of A, sew a few stitches to secure Legs.

Write or print an inspirational message on card stock and cut to desired size. Use hot glue or double-sided tape to attach sign to hands.

Weave in ends.

HOT DOG

This amigurumi hot dog is filled with an "a-bun-dance" of fun and whimsy! He's a cute reminder that you should always relish the moment, and frankly, we couldn't agree more!

AFFIRMATIONS for THE HOT DOG

I relish spending time with you!

Live with a-bun-dance.

I'll be frank. You're the best.

No one can ketchup with you.

Measurements
4" (10.2 cm) × 2½" (6.4 cm)

Yarn
Worsted weight (#4 medium)

Shown here: Lion Brand Vanna's Choice, 170 yd (156 m), 3 ½ oz (100 g), 100% acrylic: 1 ball each 860-113 Scarlet (A), and 860-158I Mustard (C)

Lion Brand Basic Stitch Anti Pilling, 185 yd (170 m), 3 ½ oz (100 g), 100% acrylic: 1 ball 202-134U Honey (B)

Hook
US Size G/6 (4 mm) crochet hook. Adjust hook size if necessary to work tightly.

Gauge
Exact gauge is not critical for this piece. Work tightly to ensure stuffing does not show through.

Notions
Yarn needle
Polyester stuffing
Black embroidery thread
Black craft wire
1 pair 6 mm black safety eyes
Scissors
Stitch marker
Card stock
Hot glue or double-sided tape

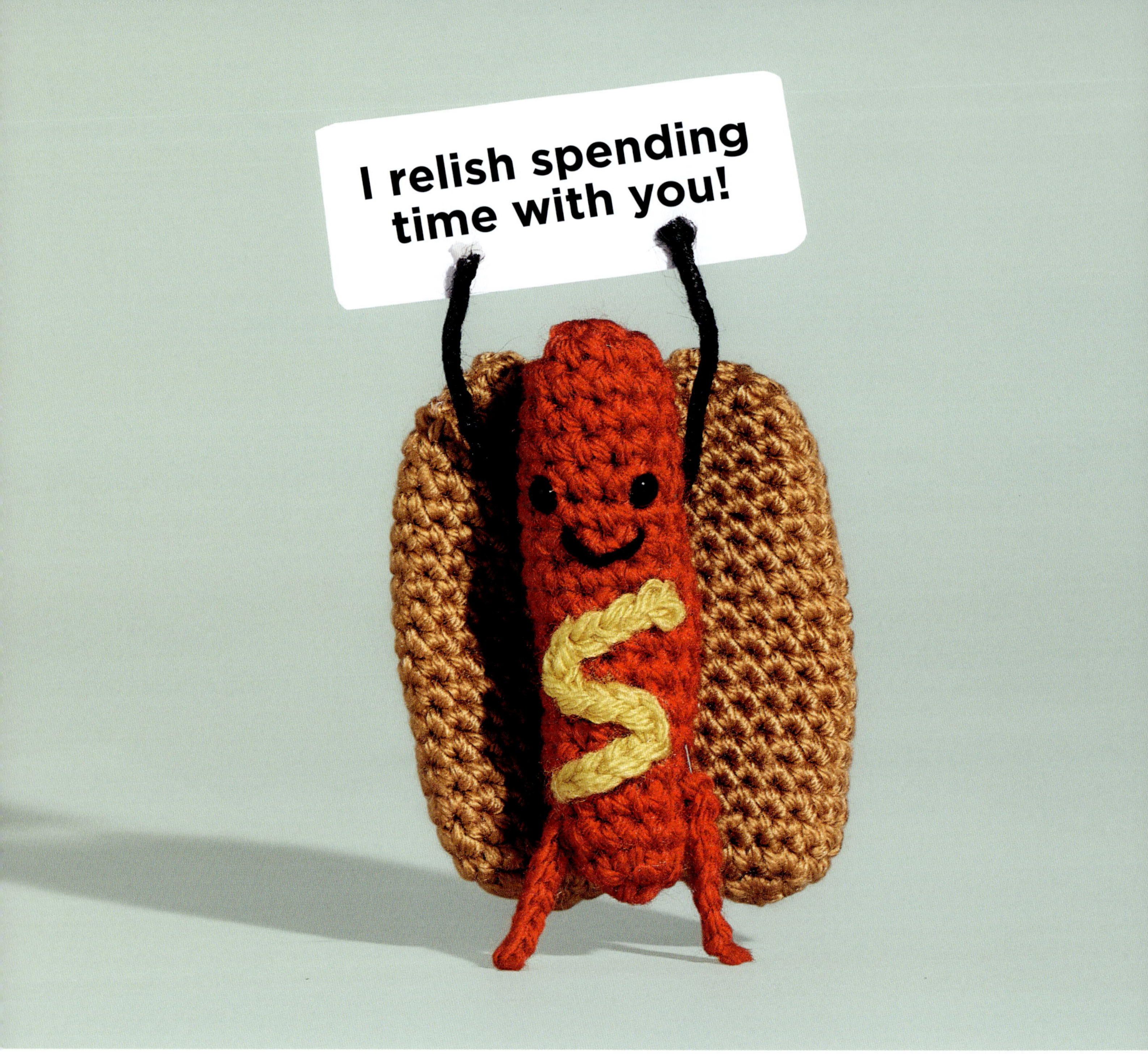
I relish spending
time with you!

Hot Dog

With A, ch 2.

Rnd 1: Work 6 sc in 2nd ch from hook; do not join. Work in continuous rnds—6 sc.

Place marker in last sc made to indicate end of rnd. Move marker up as each rnd is completed.

Rnd 2: Work 2 sc in each st around—12 sc.

Rnds 3–17: Sc around.

Add safety eyes between Rnds 6 and 7, about 2 sts apart.

Rnd 18: Inv-dec around—6 sc.

Fasten off, leaving a long tail for sewing. Sew remaining 6 sts closed.

Bun (Make 2)

With B, ch 2.

Rnd 1: Work 6 sc in 2nd ch from hook; do not join. Work in continuous rnds—6 sc.

Place marker in last sc made to indicate end of rnd. Move marker up as each rnd is completed.

Rnd 2: Work 2 sc in each st around—12 sc.

Rnd 3: [2 sc in next st, sc in next st] around—18 sc.

Rnds 4–19: Sc in each st around.

Stuff Bun lightly.

Rnd 20: [Inv-dec, sc in next st] around—12 sc.

Rnd 21: Inv-dec around—6 sc.

Fasten off, leaving a long tail for sewing. Sew remaining 6 sts closed.

Legs (Make 1)

With A, ch 20.

Fasten off and trim ends.

Mustard

With C, ch 15.

Fasten off, leaving a long tail for sewing.

Finishing

Using yarn tails, sew Buns together along one long edge.

Using black embroidery thread, embroider a smile on Hot Dog in a V shape below the eyes.

Cut a piece of black craft wire about 3½ to 4 times as long as the width of the Hot Dog. Gently poke the wire through center of Hot Dog at arm level, leaving equal-length ends sticking out of sides for arms.

Thread Legs through bottom of Hot Dog, leaving equal-length ends of ch-20 hanging down for legs. With a length of A, sew a few stitches to secure Legs.

Sew Mustard in a squiggle on top of Hot Dog.

Place Hot Dog between Buns and sew in place.

Write or print an inspirational message on card stock and cut to desired size. Use hot glue or double-sided tape to attach sign to hands.

Weave in ends.

FRiED EGG

Looking on the bright side of things can sometimes be difficult, but we hope this little cutie helps a bit! Made in beginner-friendly crochet stitches, you'll have this pattern over-easier than you can say "sunny side up"!

AFFIRMATIONS for the FRIED EGG

Keep on the sunny side.

Egg-cellent things are coming your way.

You're the best, and that's no yolk.

You're doing an egg-ceptional job.

You crack me up.

You're egg-straordinary.

Measurements

4" (10.2 cm) × 4½" (11.4 cm)

Yarn

Worsted weight (#4 medium)

Shown here: Lion Brand Vanna's Choice, 170 yd (156 m), 3½ oz (100 g), 100% acrylic: 1 ball each 860-100 White (A), and 860-158I Mustard (B)

Hook

US Size G/6 (4 mm) crochet hook. Adjust hook size if necessary to work tightly.

Gauge

Exact gauge is not critical for this piece. Work tightly to ensure stuffing does not show through.

Notions

Yarn needle
Polyester stuffing
Black embroidery thread
Black craft wire
1 pair 6 mm black safety eyes
Pink blush
Scissors
Stitch marker
Card stock
Hot glue or double-sided tape

Keep on the sunny side.

Body (Make 2)

With A, ch 4.

Row 1: Sc in 2nd ch from hook, sc in next 2 ch, turn—3 sc.

Row 2: Ch 1, 2 sc in next st, sc in next st, 2 sc in last st, turn—5 sc.

Row 3: Ch 1, 2 sc in next st, sc in each st to last 2 sts, 2 sc in each of last 2 sts, turn—8 sc.

Row 4: Ch 1, 2 sc in each of next 2 sts, sc in each st to last st, 2 sc in last st, turn—11 sc.

Rows 5 and 6: Rep Rows 3 and 4—17 sc in Row 6.

Row 7: Ch 1, 2 sc in each of next 2 sts, sc in each st across, turn—19 sc.

Rows 8 and 9: Ch 1, sc in each st to last 2 sts, 2 sc in each of last 2 sts, turn—23 sc in Row 9.

Row 10: Ch 1, 2 sc in each of next 2 sts, sc in each st across, turn—25 sc.

Rows 11 and 12: Ch 1, [sc2tog] 2 times, sc in each st to last 4 sts, [sc2tog] 2 times, turn—17 sc in Row 12.

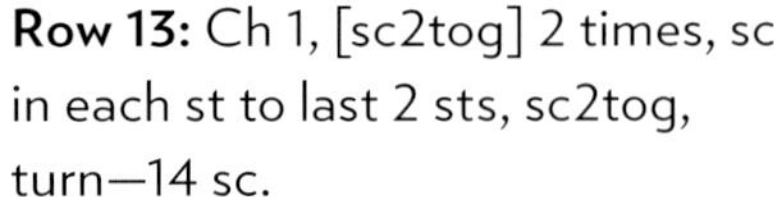

Row 13: Ch 1, [sc2tog] 2 times, sc in each st to last 2 sts, sc2tog, turn—14 sc.

Row 14: Ch 1, sc in each st to last 4 sts, [sc2tog] 2 times, turn—12 sc.

Row 15: Ch 1, sc in each st across, turn.

Row 16: Ch 1, sc in each st to last 2 sts, 2 sc in each of last 2 sts, turn—14 sc.

Row 17: Ch 1, 2 sc in each of next 2 sts, sc in each st across, turn—16 sc.

Row 18: Ch 1, [sc2tog] 2 times, sc in each st across, turn—14 sc.

Row 19: Ch 1, [sc2tog] 2 times, sc in next 3 sts, sc2tog, turn, leaving remaining 5 sts unworked—6 sc.

Row 20: Ch 1, [sc2tog] 3 times, turn—3 sc.

Row 21: Ch 1, sc in next st, sc2tog—2 sc.

Fasten off.

Row 22: Draw up a loop of A in next unworked st of Row 19, ch 1, sc in same st, [sc2tog] 2 times, turn—3 sc.

Row 23: Ch 1, sc in next st, sc2tog—2 sc.

Fasten off.

Border

Hold 2 Body pieces with RS of front piece facing you and edges matching.

Rnd 1: Working through both thicknesses and beg along opposite side of foundation ch, draw up a loop of A in ch at base of first sc, ch 1, sc evenly spaced all the way around outer edge of Body, working 2 sc in each "peak"; join with sl st in first sc.

Fasten off.

Yolk

With B, ch 2.

Rnd 1: Work 6 sc in 2nd ch from hook; do not join, work in continuous rnds—6 sc.

Place a marker in last sc made to indicate end of rnd. Move marker up as each rnd is completed.

Rnd 2: 2 sc in each st around—12 sc.

Rnd 3: [2 sc in next st, sc in next st] around—18 sc.

Rnd 4: Sc in each st around.

Fasten off, leaving a long tail for sewing. Add safety eyes between Rnds 2 and 3, about 2 to 3 sts apart.

Finishing

Cut 2 pieces of black craft wire a little shorter than the width of the Body. Wrap one end of each piece around a stitch or two on either side edge of Body at arm level for arms.

Using black embroidery thread, embroider a smile in a V shape below the eyes.

Add a small amount of blush under each eye.

Write or print an inspirational message on card stock and cut to desired size. Use hot glue or double-sided tape to attach sign to hands.

Weave in ends.

Nothing is im-popsicle!

POPSICLE

We think you're absolutely dripping with style and pizzazz, just like this wee crocheted popsicle friend! Made in the classic rocket-pop colors, this adorable treat will remind you to stay cool and enjoy the sunshine!

AFFIRMATIONS for the POPSICLE

Nothing is im-popsicle!

Chill out, you're crushing it!

Stick with it!

Keep cool.

Spending time with you is a treat.

Measurements
5" (12.7 cm) × 2½" (6.4 cm)

Yarn
Worsted weight (#4 medium)

Shown here: Lion Brand Vanna's Choice, 170 yd (156 m), 3½ oz (100 g), 100% acrylic: 1 ball each 860-113 Scarlet (A), 860-100 White (B), and 860-109E Colonial Blue (C)

Lion Brand Basic Stitch Anti Pilling, 185 yd (170 m), 3½ oz (100 g), 100% acrylic: 1 ball 202-102W Clay (D)

Hook
US Size G/6 (4 mm) crochet hook. Adjust hook size if necessary to work tightly.

Gauge
Exact gauge is not critical for this piece. Work tightly to ensure stuffing does not show through.

Notions
Yarn needle
Polyester stuffing
Black embroidery thread
Black craft wire
1 pair 6 mm black safety eyes
Scissors
Stitch marker
Card stock
Hot glue or double-sided tape

Body

With A, ch 2.

Rnd 1: Work 6 sc in 2nd ch from hook; do not join, work in continuous rnds—6 sc.

Place a marker in last sc made to indicate end of rnd. Move marker up as each rnd is completed.

Rnd 2: Work 2 sc in each st around—12 sc.

Rnd 3: [Sc in next 3 sts, 2 sc in each of next 3 sts] around—18 sc.

Rnd 4: * Sc in next 3 sts, [2 sc in next st, sc in next st] 3 times; rep from * around—24 sc.

Rnd 5: * Sc in next 3 sts, [sc in next st, 2 sc in next st, sc in next st] 3 times; rep from * around—30 sc.

Rnds 6 and 7: Sc in each st around.

Rnd 8: Sc in each st around; join with sl st in first sc.

Change to B.

Rnd 9: Working in BLO, ch 1, sc in each st around, join with sl st in first sc.

Rnd 10: Ch 1 tightly, sc in each st around, do not join.

Rnds 11–13: Sc in each st around.

Rnd 14: Sc in each st around; join with sl st in first sc.

Change to C.

Rnds 15–20: Rep Rnds 9–14.

Fasten off. Add safety eyes between Rnds 11 and 12, about 4 sts apart.

Bottom

With D, ch 2.

Rnd 1: Work 6 sc in 2nd ch from hook; do not join, work in continuous rnds—6 sc.

Place a marker in last sc made to indicate end of rnd. Move marker up as each rnd is completed.

Rnd 2: [2 sc in next st, sc in next st] around—9 sc.

Rnds 3–7: Sc in each st around.

Change to C.

Rnd 8: Ch 1, [2 sc in next st, sc in next 2 sts] around; join with sl st in first sc—12 sc.

Rnd 9: Ch 1 tightly, [sc in next 3 sts, 2 sc in each of next 3 sts] around, do not join, work remainder of piece in continuous rnds—18 sc.

Rnd 10: * Sc in next 3 sts, [2 sc in next st, sc in next st] 3 times; rep from * around—24 sc.

Rnd 11: *Sc in next 3 sts, [sc in next st, 2 sc in next st, sc in next st] 3 times; rep from * around—30 sc.

Fasten off, leaving a long tail for sewing.

Finishing

Stuff Body. Sew Bottom to Body.

Using black embroidery thread, embroider a smile in a V shape between the eyes.

Cut a piece of black craft wire about 2½ to 3 times as long as the width of the piece. Gently poke the wire through center of piece at arm level, leaving equal-length ends sticking out of sides for arms.

Write or print an inspirational message on card stock and cut to desired size. Use hot glue or double-sided tape to attach sign to hands.

Weave in ends.

PINEAPPLE

We all pine for those special moments with our besties. The piña to our colada, the pine-apple of our eye! Besties are so sweet and deserve it all. You can crochet this adorable pineapple for your bestie and remind them to stand tall and wear a crown.

AFFIRMATIONS for the PINEAPPLE

You're the pine-apple of my eye.

You're tough on the outside, but sweet on the inside.

Stand tall and wear a crown.

May you live pineapple-y ever after.

Measurements

4½" (11.4 cm) × 3" (12.7cm)

Yarn

Worsted weight (#4 medium)

Shown here: Lion Brand Vanna's Choice, 170 yd (156 m), 3½ oz (100 g), 100% acrylic: 1 ball each 860-158I Mustard (A) and 860-172C Kelly Green (B)

Hook

US Size G/6 (4 mm) crochet hook. Adjust hook size if necessary to work tightly.

Gauge

Exact gauge is not critical for this piece. Work tightly to ensure stuffing does not show through.

Notions

Yarn needle
Polyester stuffing
Black embroidery thread
Black craft wire
1 pair 6 mm black safety eyes
Pink blush
Scissors
Stitch marker
Card stock
Hot glue or double-sided tape

Special Stitch

Cluster (2-sc cluster)= [Insert hook in indicated st, yarn over and draw up a loop, yarn over and draw through 1 loop on hook] 2 times, yarn over and draw through 3 remaining loops.

You're the pine-apple
of my eye.

Body

With A, ch 2.

Rnd 1: Work 6 sc in 2nd ch from hook; do not join. Work in continuous rnds—6 sc.

Place marker in last sc made to indicate end of rnd. Move marker up as each rnd is completed.

Rnd 2: Work 2 sc in each st around—12 sc.

Rnd 3: [2 sc in next st, sc in next st] around—18 sc.

Rnd 4: [Cluster in next st, 2 clusters in next st, cluster in next st] around—24 clusters.

Rnd 5: [2 sc in next st, sc in next 3 sts] around—30 sc.

Rnd 6: Cluster in each st around—30 clusters.

Rnd 7: Sc in each st around.

Rnds 8–13: Rep Rnds 6 and 7.

Rnd 14: Rep Rnd 6.

Rnd 15: [Inv-dec, sc in next 3 sts] around—24 sc.

Add safety eyes between Rnds 9 and 10, about 4 sts apart.

Stuff Body and continue stuffing as work progresses.

Rnd 16: [Cluster in next st, inv-dec, cluster in next st] around—12 clusters and 6 sc.

Rnd 17: [Inv-dec, sc in next st] around—12 sc.

Rnd 18: Working in BLO, sc2tog around—6 sc.

Fasten off, leaving a long tail for sewing. Sew remaining 6 sts closed.

Leaves

Draw up a loop of B in FLO of Rnd 17 at back of Body.

Rnd 1: Ch 1, sc in each st around; join with sl st in first sc—12 sc.

Rnd 2: * Ch 10, sc in 2nd ch from hook, sc in next 2 ch, hdc in next 3 ch, dc in next 3 ch, sl st in in next st of Rnd 1; rep from * around—12 leaves.

Fasten off.

Finishing

Cut a piece of black craft wire about 2½ to 3 times as long as the width of the piece. Gently poke the wire through center of Body at arm level, leaving equal-length ends sticking out of sides for arms.

Using black embroidery thread, embroider a smile in a V shape below the eyes.

Add a small amount of blush under each eye.

Write or print an inspirational message on card stock and cut to desired size. Use hot glue or double-sided tape to attach sign to hands.

Weave in ends.

Hang in there!
If you were a dinosaur, you'd be a super-saurus!
Slow and steady wins the race.
Feline good!

CHAPTER 3

ANIMAL ALLIES & CARING CRITTERS

This chapter is all about bringing crochet animals to life! From a loyal puppy to a whimsical snail to a sweet dragon, these lovable creatures will warm your heart. Let's create some charming animal pals, each ready to spread joy wherever they go!

Keep on
cluckin'!

CHICKEN

This emotional support chicken is here to remind you that you're never alone in the tough moments. With its fluffy feathers and comforting presence, this little chicken offers warmth, encouragement, and a gentle reminder that everything will be okay.

AFFIRMATIONS for THE CHICKEN

Keep on cluckin'!

Don't get your feathers ruffled.

You're one cool chick.

Friends like you are as scarce as hen's teeth.

You've hatched into greatness.

Let's get together and hatch a plan.

Measurements
3½" (8.9 cm) × 2" (5.1 cm)

Yarn
Worsted weight (#4 medium)

Shown here: WeCrochet Brava Worsted 218 yd (200 m), 3½ oz (100 g), 100% acrylic: 1 ball each 28455 White (A), 28445 Red (B), and 28417 Caution (C)

Hook
US Size G/6 (4 mm) crochet hook. Adjust hook size if necessary to work tightly.

Gauge
Exact gauge is not critical for this piece. Work tightly to ensure stuffing does not show through.

Notions
Yarn needle
Polyester stuffing
1 pair 6 mm black safety eyes
Scissors
Stitch marker
Card stock
Hot glue or double-sided tape

Special Stitch
Cluster (2-dc cluster) = [Yarn over, insert hook in indicated st, yarn over and draw up a loop, yarn over and draw through 2 loops on hook] 2 times, yarn over and draw through 3 remaining loops.

Body

With A, ch 6.

Rnd 1: Sc in 2nd ch from hook and in next 3 ch, 3 sc in last ch; working along opposite side of foundation ch, sc in next 4 ch, 3 sc in last ch (ch that was skipped at beg of rnd); do not join, work in continuous rnds—14 sc.

Place a marker in last sc made to indicate end of rnd. Move marker up as each rnd is completed.

Rnd 2: [Sc in next 4 sts, 2 sc in each of next 3 sts] 2 times—20 sc.

Rnd 3: * Sc in next 4 sts, [2 sc in next st, sc in next st] 3 times; rep from * once more—26 sc.

Rnd 4: Sc in next 4 sts, [2 sc in next st, sc in next 2 sts] 3 times, sc in next 13 sts—29 sc.

Rnd 5: Sc in next 10 sts, 3 sc in next st, sc in next 18 sts—31 sc.

Rnd 6: Sc in next 11 sts, 3 sc in next st, sc in next 19 sts—33 sc.

Rnd 7: Sc in next 12 sts, 3 sc in next st, sc in next 20 sts—35 sc.

Rnd 8: Sc in next 13 sts, 3 sc in next st, sc in next 21 sts—37 sc.

Rnd 9: Sc in next 14 sts, 3 sc in next st, sc in next 22 sts—39 sc.

Rnds 10 and 11: Sc in each st around.

Do not fasten off. Continue to head.

Head

Rnd 1: Sc in next 5 sts, sk next 21 sts, sc in next 13 sts—18 sc.

Rnds 2–4: Sc in each st around.

Rnd 5: [Inv-dec, sc in next st] around—12 sc.

Rnd 6: Inv-dec around—6 sc.

Fasten off, leaving a long tail for sewing. Sew remaining 6 sts closed. Add eyes between Rnds 1 and 2 on either side of head.

Crest

With B, ch 5.

Row 1: Beg in 2nd ch from hook, [Cluster in next ch, sk next ch] 2 times, Cluster in last ch—3 Clusters.

Fasten off, leaving a long tail for sewing.

Beak

With C, ch 3.

Row 1: Sc in 2nd ch from hook, dc in last ch—2 sts.

Fasten off, leaving a long tail for sewing.

Wings (Make 2)

With A, ch 2.

Rnd 1: Work 6 sc in 2nd ch from hook; do not join, work in continuous rnds—6 sc.

Rnd 2: 2 sc in each st around—12 sc.

Next (partial) rnd: (Sl st, ch 6, sl st) in each of next 3 sts—3 ch-6 sps.

Fasten off, leaving a long tail for sewing.

Legs (Make 1)

With C, ch 20.

Fasten off and trim ends.

Finishing

Stuff Body.

Using a long piece of A, sew back seam closed.

Sew Crest to top of head.

Sew Wings to either side of Body.

Thread Legs through bottom of Body, leaving equal-length ends of ch-20 hanging down for legs. With a length of A, sew a few stitches to secure Legs.

Sew Beak to front of head.

Write or print an inspirational message on card stock and cut to desired size. Use hot glue or double-sided tape to attach sign to a Wing.

Weave in ends.

CAT

If you need any indication that a kitty thinks you are the "cat's meow," look for the signs. A reassuring brush against your legs and an adorable purr mean your cat thinks you are nothing but purr-fect.

AFFIRMATIONS for THE CAT

You're the cat's meow.

I'm not kitten around, you're the best!

You've got cat-titude.

Don't stress meow-t.

You have purr-sonality.

Measurements
4½" (11.4 cm) × 2" (5.1 cm)

Yarn
Worsted weight (#4 medium)

Shown here: Lion Brand Wool Ease, 197 yd (180 m), 3 oz (85 g), 80% acrylic/20% wool: 1 ball each 620-151 Grey Heather (A) and 620-052 Flint (B)

Hook
US Size G/6 (4 mm) crochet hook. Adjust hook size if necessary to work tightly.

Gauge
Exact gauge is not critical for this piece. Work tightly to ensure stuffing does not show through.

Notions
Yarn needle
Polyester stuffing
Pink embroidery thread
Black embroidery thread
White embroidery thread
1 pair 6 mm black safety eyes
Scissors
Stitch marker
Card stock
Hot glue or double-sided tape

You're the
cat's meow.

Front Legs (Make 2)

With A, make a magic loop.

Rnd 1: Work 6 sc in loop; do not join. Work in continuous rnds—6 sc.

Place marker in last sc made to indicate end of rnd. Move marker up as each rnd is completed.

Rnd 2: Work 2 sc in each of next 3 sts, sc in next 3 sts—9 sc.

Rnd 3: Sc in each st around.

Stuff Front Leg and continue stuffing as work progresses.

Rnd 4: [Inv-dec] 3 times, sc in next 3 sts—6 sc.

Rnds 5–9: Sc in each st around.

Fasten off.

Body

With A, make a magic loop.

Rnd 1: Work 6 sc in loop; do not join. Work in continuous rnds—6 sc.

Place marker in last sc made to indicate end of rnd. Move marker up as each rnd is completed.

Rnd 2: Work 2 sc in each st around—12 sc.

Rnd 3: [2 sc in next st, sc in next st] around—18 sc.

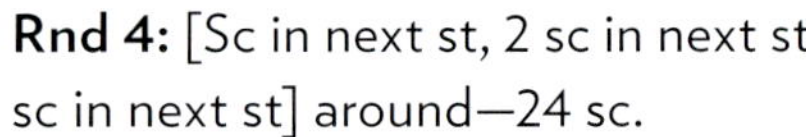

Rnd 4: [Sc in next st, 2 sc in next st, sc in next st] around—24 sc.

Rnds 5–10: Sc in each st around.

Rnd 11 (Join Front Legs): Sc in next 3 sts; beg at back of first Front Leg, sc in each st of Leg, sc in next 3 sts of Rnd 10; beg at back of 2nd Front Leg, sc in each st of Leg, sc in next 18 sts of Rnd 10—36 sc.

Rnds 12 and 13: Sc in each st around.

Rnd 14: Inv-dec, sc in next 19 sts, [inv-dec, sc in next st] 5 times—30 sc.

Rnds 15 and 16: Sc in each st around.

Rnd 17: [Inv-dec, sc in next 3 sts] around—24 sc.

Rnd 18: [Sc in next st, inv-dec, sc in next st] around—18 sc.

Stuff Body and continue stuffing as work progresses.

Rnd 19: [Inv-dec, sc in next st] around—12 sc.

Do not fasten off. Continue to Head.

Head

Rnd 1: Continuing with A, 3 sc in each st around—36 sc.

Rnds 2–7: Sc in each st around.

Rnd 8: [Sc in next st, inv-dec, sc in next st] around—27 sc.

Rnd 9: [Inv-dec, sc in next 7 sts] around—24 sc.

Rnds 10 and 11: Sc in each st around.

Add safety eyes between Rnds 8 and 9, about 3 to 4 sts apart. Stuff Head and continue stuffing as work progresses.

Rnd 12: [Sc in next st, inv-dec, sc in next st] around—18 sc.

Rnd 13: [Inv-dec, sc in next st] around—12 sc.

Rnd 14: Inv-dec around—6 sc.

Fasten off, leaving a long tail for sewing. Sew remaining 6 sts closed.

Back Legs (Make 2)

With A, make a magic loop.

Rnds 1–5: Work same as Rnds 1–5 of Front Legs—6 sc.

Rnd 6: [2 sc in next st, sc in next st] around—9 sc.

Rnds 7 and 8: Sc in each st around.

Stuff Back Leg and continue stuffing as work progresses.

Rnd 9: [Inv-dec, sc in next st] 3 times—6 sc

Fasten off, leaving a long tail for sewing.

Ears (Make 2— 1 each with A and B)

Make a magic loop.

Rnd 1: Work 3 sc in loop; do not join. Work in continuous rnds—3 sc.

Place marker in last sc made to indicate end of rnd. Move marker up as each rnd is completed.

Rnd 2: 2 sc in next st, sc in next 2 sts—4 sc.

Rnd 3: [2 sc in next st, sc in next st] around—6 sc.

Rnd 4: [2 sc in next st, sc in next st] around—9 sc.

Fasten off, leaving a long tail for sewing.

Muzzle

With A, make a magic loop.

Rnd 1: Work 6 sc in loop; do not join. Work in continuous rnds—6 sc.

Place marker in last sc made to indicate end of rnd. Move marker up as each rnd is completed.

Rnd 2: Work 2 sc in each st around—12 sc.

Rnd 3: Sc in each st around.

Fasten off, leaving a long tail for sewing.

Tail

With B, make a magic loop.

Rnd 1: Work 6 sc in loop; do not join. Work in continuous rnds—6 sc.

Place marker in last sc made to indicate end of rnd. Move marker up as each rnd is completed.

Rnds 2–31: Sc in each st around.

Fasten off, leaving a long tail for sewing.

Finishing

Sew Back Legs to either side of Body.

Sew Ears to top of Head.

Sew Tail to back of Body.

Using pink embroidery thread, embroider a triangle nose on Muzzle.

Sew Muzzle to front of Head under eyes.

Using black embroidery thread, embroider 3 whiskers on either side of Muzzle.

Using white embroidery thread, embroider 3 lines for claws on each paw.

Write or print an inspirational message on card stock and cut to desired size. Use hot glue or double-sided tape to attach sign to Cat.

Weave in ends.

You are
dino-mite!

DINOSAUR

What's your favorite dinosaur? I had so many to choose from for this book, and I felt like a brontosaurus would be so kind and encouraging. A gentle giant with a friendly little face. He'd be happy to hang out with you and watch the clouds all day, which honestly sounds dino-mite.

AFFIRMATIONS for THE DINOSAUR

You are dino-mite!

If you were a dinosaur, you'd be a super-saurus!

You're pterrific!

I dino what I'd do without you.

I feel like I've known you for a million years.

Measurements
4½" (11.4 cm) × 1½" (3.8 cm)

Yarn
Worsted weight (#4 medium)

Shown here: Lion Brand Vanna's Choice, 170 yd (156 m), 3½ oz (100 g), 100% acrylic: 1 ball 860-172C Kelly Green

Hook
US Size G/6 (4 mm) crochet hook. Adjust hook size if necessary to work tightly.

Gauge
Exact gauge is not critical for this piece. Work tightly to ensure stuffing does not show through.

Notions
Yarn needle
Polyester stuffing
1 pair 6 mm black safety eyes
Scissors
Stitch marker
Card stock
Hot glue or double-sided tape

Feet (Make 4)

Make a magic loop.

Rnd 1: Work 6 sc in loop; join with sl st in first sc—6 sc.

Rnd 2: Ch 1, working in BLO, sc in each st around; join with sl st in first sc.

Rnd 3: Ch 1, sc in each st around; join with sl st in first sc.

Fasten off. Stuff Feet.

Body

Ch 5.

Rnd 1: Sc in 2nd ch from hook, sc in next 2 ch, 3 sc in last ch; working along opposite side of foundation ch, sc in next 3 ch, 3 sc in next ch (ch that was skipped at beg of rnd); join with sl st in first sc—12 sc.

Rnd 2: Ch 1, [sc in next 3 sts, 2 sc in each of next 3 sts] 2 times; join with sl st in first sc—18 sc.

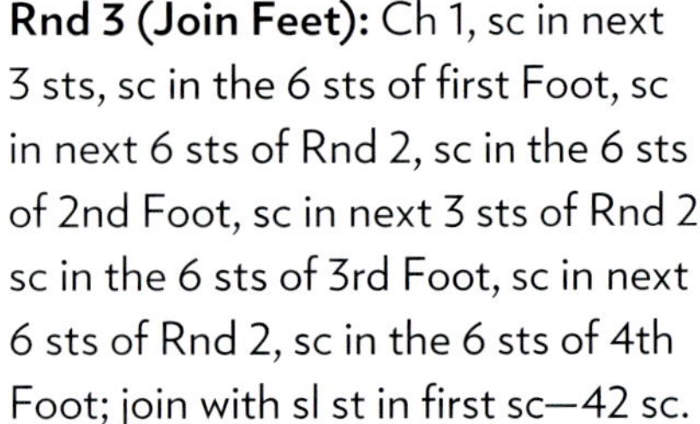

Rnd 3 (Join Feet): Ch 1, sc in next 3 sts, sc in the 6 sts of first Foot, sc in next 6 sts of Rnd 2, sc in the 6 sts of 2nd Foot, sc in next 3 sts of Rnd 2, sc in the 6 sts of 3rd Foot, sc in next 6 sts of Rnd 2, sc in the 6 sts of 4th Foot; join with sl st in first sc—42 sc.

Rnds 4–8: Ch 1, sc in each st around; join with sl st in first sc.

Rnd 9: Ch 1, sc in next 20 sts, ch 6, sk next 6 sts (tail opening made), sc in last 16 sts; join with sl st in first sc—36 sc, 1 ch-6 sp.

Rnd 10: Ch 1, [sc in next 5 sts, sc2tog] around; join with sl st in first sc—36 sc.

Rnd 11: Ch 1, sc in each st around; join with sl st in first sc.

Rnd 12 (Neck): Ch 1, sc in next 9 sts, sk next 24 sts, sc in next 3 sts; join with sl st in first sc—12 sc.

Rnds 13: Ch 1, sc in each st around, do not join, begin working in continuous rnds.

Place a marker in last sc made to indicate end of rnd. Move marker up as each rnd is completed.

Rnds 14 and 15: Sc in each st around.

Rnd 16: [Inv-dec, sc in next 2 sts] around—9 sc.

Rnds 17–20: Sc in each st around.

Rnd 21: Sc in next 2 sts, 2 sc in next 3 sts, sc in next 4 sts—12 sc.

Rnd 22: Sc in next 2 sts, [2 sc in next st, sc in next st] 3 times, sc in next 4 sts—15 sc.

Rnd 23: Sc in next 2 sts, [sc in next st, 2 sc in next st, sc in next st] 3 times, sc in next 4 sts—18 sc.

Rnd 24: Sc in next 2 sts, [2 sc in next st, sc in next 3 sts] 3 times, sc in next 4 sts—21 sc.

Rnds 25 and 26: Sc in each st around.

Rnd 27: Sc in next 6 sts, [inv-dec] 3 times, sc in next 9 sts—18 sc.

Add safety eyes between Rnds 25 and 26. Stuff Body and continue stuffing as work progresses.

Rnd 28: [Sc in next st, inv-dec] around—12 sc.

Rnd 29: Inv-dec around—6 sc.

Fasten off, leaving a long tail for sewing. Sew remaining 6 sts closed.

Tail

Draw up a loop of yarn in first skipped sc of Rnd 8 of Body.

Rnd 1: Beg in same st as joining, sc in next 5 sts, sc2tog over next sc and gap before ch-6 space, sc in underside of next 5 ch, sc2tog over next ch and gap before first sc; do not join, work in continuous rnds—12 sc.

Place a marker in last sc made to indicate end of rnd. Move marker up as each rnd is completed.

Rnds 2–4: Sc in each st around.

Rnd 5: [Inv-dec, sc in next 2 sts] around—9 sc.

Rnds 6–8: Sc in each st around.

Rnd 9: Inv-dec, sc in each st around—8 sc.

Rnds 10 and 11: Sc in each st around.

Rnd 12: Inv-dec, sc in each st around—7 sc.

Rnds 13–15: Rep Rnds 10–12—6 sc in Rnd 15.

Stuff Tail and continue stuffing as work progresses.

Rnds 16–21: Rep Rnds 10–12 twice—4 sc in Rnd 21.

Rnds 22 and 23: Sc in each st around.

Fasten off, leaving a long tail for sewing. Sew remaining 4 sts closed.

Finishing

Using a length of A, sew back seam closed.

Using a length of A, sew small gap at top of each Foot closed.

Write or print an inspirational message on card stock and cut to desired size. Use hot glue or double-sided tape to attach sign to Dinosaur.

Weave in ends.

You're making progress at your own pace.

SNAIL

They say "slow and steady wins the race," and if that's true, this little snail friend is a winner in our books! With a colorful, speckled shell and a cute little face, this adorable guy is a healthy reminder to slow down and enjoy the little things in life.

AFFIRMATIONS for THE SNAIL

You're making progress at your own pace.

Keep moving toward your goals.

You're at home wherever you go.

Keep calm and carry on.

Slow and steady wins the race.

Measurements
4½" (11.4 cm) × 1½" (3.8 cm)

Yarn
Worsted weight (#4 medium)

Shown here: WeCrochet Brava Speckle 218 yd (200 m), 3½ oz (100 g), 100% acrylic: 1 skein 29242 Cake Pop Speckle (A)

WeCrochet Brava Worsted 218 yd (200 m), 3½ oz (100 g), 100% acrylic: 1 ball 28423 Cotton Candy (B)

Hook
US Size G/6 (4 mm) crochet hook. Adjust hook size if necessary to work tightly.

Gauge
Exact gauge is not critical for this piece. Work tightly to ensure stuffing does not show through.

Notions
Yarn needle
Polyester stuffing
Black embroidery thread
1 pair 6 mm black safety eyes
Scissors
Stitch marker
Card stock
Hot glue or double-sided tape

Shell

With A, ch 2.

Rnd 1: Work 6 sc in 2nd ch from hook; do not join, work in continuous rnds—6 sc.

Place a marker in last sc made to indicate end of rnd. Move marker up as each rnd is completed.

Rnd 2: [2 sc in next st, sc in next st] around—9 sc.

Rnd 3: [Sc in next st, 2 sc in next st, sc in next st] around—12 sc.

Rnds 4–67: Sc in each st around.

Fasten off, leaving a long tail for sewing.

Body

With B, ch 2.

Rnd 1: Work 6 sc in 2nd ch from hook; do not join, work in continuous rnds—6 sc.

Place a marker in last sc made to indicate end of rnd. Move marker up as each rnd is completed.

Rnd 2: Work 2 sc in each st around—12 sc.

Rnd 3: [2 sc in next st, sc in next st] around—18 sc.

Rnd 4: [Sc in next st, 2 sc in next st, sc in next st] around—24 sc.

Rnds 5–8: Sc in each st around.

Rnd 9: [Sc in next st, inv-dec, sc in next st] around—18 sc.

Add safety eyes between Rnds 5 and 6, about 4 sts apart. Stuff Body and continue stuffing as work progresses.

Rnd 10: [Inv-dec, sc in next st] around—12 sc.

Rnd 11: Inv-dec around—6 sc.

Rnd 12: 2 sc in each st around—12 sc.

Rnds 13–28: Sc in each st around.

Rnd 29: [Inv-dec, sc next 2 sts] around—9 sc.

Rnd 30: Sc in each st around.

Rnd 31: [Inv-dec, sc in next st] around—6 sc.

Rnd 32: Sc in each st around.

Fasten off, leaving a long tail for sewing. Sew the remaining 6 sc closed.

Body Lining

With B, ch 35.

Row 1: Work 2 sc in 2nd ch from hook, 2 sc in each ch across—68 sc.

Fasten off, leaving a long tail for sewing.

Antenna (Make 2)

With B, ch 2.

Rnd 1: Work 4 sc in 2nd ch from hook; do not join, work in continuous rnds—4 sc.

Place a marker in last sc made to indicate end of rnd. Move marker up as each rnd is completed.

Rnd 2: [2 sc in next st, sc in next st] around—6 sc.

Rnds 3 and 4: Sc in each st around.

Rnd 5: Inv-dec around—3 sc.

Rnd 6: Ch 6, sc in 2nd ch from hook, sc in next 4 ch, sl st in next st of Rnd 5, ch 1; working along opposite side of the ch-6, sl st in next 5 ch—5 sc.

Fasten off, leaving a long tail for sewing. Fold Rnd 6 in half lengthwise, matching the sc along one side and sl st along other side. Sew 5 sl sts to 5 sc sts of Rnd 6.

Finishing

Curl Shell into a flat spiral, sewing layers together as spiral grows.

Sew Shell to top of Body, below head.

Using photographs as a guide, sew Body Lining around lower edge of Body.

Sew Antennae to top of head.

Using black embroidery thread, embroider a smile in a V shape below the eyes.

Write or print an inspirational message on card stock and cut to desired size. Use hot glue or double-sided tape to attach sign to Snail.

Weave in ends.

OWL

Owls are wise, we all know that. So when this owl tells you that you are smart and kind and loving, you just have to believe it's true. This cute little owl showcases some classic crochet styling we all loved as beginners, reminding us all how far we've come.

AFFIRMATIONS for THE OWL

You're owl that.

You are wise beyond measure.

I don't give a hoot!

I'm owl-ways here for you.

Measurements
5" (12.7 cm) × 5" (12.7 cm)

Yarn
Worsted weight (#4 medium)

Shown here: Lion Brand Basic Stitch Anti Pilling, 185 yd (170 m), 3½ oz (100 g), 100% acrylic: 1 ball each 202-112S Deco Rose (A), 202-100 White (B), 202-158I Mustard (C), and 202-110AW Stonewash (D)

Hook
US Size G/6 (4 mm) crochet hook. Adjust hook size if necessary to work tightly.

Gauge
Exact gauge is not critical for this piece. Work tightly to ensure stuffing does not show through.

Notions
Yarn needle
Polyester stuffing
1 pair 12 mm black and yellow safety eyes
Scissors
Stitch marker
Card stock
Hot glue or double-sided tape

You're owl that.

Body

With A, make a magic loop.

Rnd 1: Work 6 sc in loop; do not join. Work in continuous rnds—6 sc.

Place marker in last sc made to indicate end of rnd. Move marker up as each rnd is completed.

Rnd 2: Work 2 sc in each st around—12 sc.

Rnd 3: [2 sc in next st, sc in next st] around—18 sc.

Rnd 4: [Sc in next st, 2 sc in next st, sc in next st] around—24 sc.

Rnd 5: [2 sc in next st, sc in next 3 sts] around—30 sc.

Rnd 6: [Sc in next 2 sts, 2 sc in next st, sc in next 2 sts] around—36 sc.

Rnd 7: [2 sc in next st, sc in next 5 sts] around—42 sc.

Rnd 8: Working in BLO, sc in each st around.

Rnd 9: Sc in each st around.

Rnd 10: * Sc in next st of Rnd 9, sk st in Rnd 7 directly below sc just made, dc in FLO of next st in Rnd 7 (sk the st in Rnd 9 you would usually work into); rep from * around—21 sc and 21 dc.

Rnds 11 and 12: Rep Rnds 8 and 9.

Rnd 13: * Dc in FLO of next st in Rnd 10 (sk the st in Rnd 12 you would usually work into), sc in next st of Rnd 12, sk st in Rnd 10 directly below sc just made; rep from * around—21 dc and 21 sc.

Rnds 14–19: Rep Rnds 8–13.

Rnd 20: Rep Rnd 8.

Rnds 21–24: Sc in each st around.

Rnds 25 and 26: Sc in next 4 sts, hdc in next 4 sts, dc in next 6 sts, hdc in next 4 sts, sc in next 7 sts, hdc in next 4 sts, dc in next 6 sts, hdc in next 4 sts, sc in last 3 sts—42 sts.

Fasten off, leaving a long tail for sewing.

Eye (Make 2)

With B, make a magic loop.

Rnd 1: Work 6 sc in loop; do not join. Work in continuous rnds—6 sc.

Place marker in last sc made to indicate end of rnd. Move marker up as each rnd is completed.

Rnd 2: Work 2 sc in each st around—12 sc.

Rnd 3: [2 sc in next st, sc in next st] around—18 sc.

Fasten off, leaving a long tail for sewing.

Beak

With C, ch 3.

Row 1: Sc in 2nd ch from hook, dc in last ch—2 sts.

Fasten off, leaving a long tail for sewing.

Wing (Make 2)

With D, make a magic loop.

Rnd 1: Work 6 sc in loop; do not join. Work in continuous rnds—6 sc.

Place marker in last sc made to indicate end of rnd. Move marker up as each rnd is completed.

Rnd 2: Work 2 sc in each st around—12 sc.

Rnd 3: [2 sc in next st, sc in next st] around—18 sc.

Rnd 4: [Sc in next st, 2 sc in next st, sc in next st] around—24 sc.

Rnd 5: [2 sc in next st, sc in next 3 sts] around—30 sc.

Fasten off, leaving a long tail for sewing. Pinch top of circle and use ending tail to sew 1" (2.5 cm) of edges together to cinch top of Wing.

Finishing

Insert safety eyes through center of Eyes. Secure safety eyes between Rnds 23 and 24 of Body and in line with center 7 sc of last 2 Body rnds (dc sts act as ears on sides of Body).

Using ending tail, sew Eyes down.

Sew Beak between Eyes.

Stuff Body and use ending tail to sew top seam shut.

Sew Wings to side of Body.

Hold 3 strands of D together and add them to top corners of Body for tufts.

Write or print an inspirational message on card stock and cut to desired size. Use hot glue or double-sided tape to attach sign to a Wing.

Weave in ends.

Optimistic
Octopus

OCTOPUS

Imagine eight high fives. Or a giant hug with eight arms. This sweet and supportive octopus is ready to congratulate you on getting through the day and doing your best. Whether it's a little fist bump, or eight, you deserve it.

AFFIRMATIONS for THE OCTOPUS

Optimistic Octopus

You're juggling a lot.

Need a little squeeze?

There's nothing you can't hand-le.

I'd like to be under the sea . . . with you!

Measurements
3½" (8.9 cm) × 7½" (19.1 cm)

Yarn
Worsted weight (#4 medium)

Shown here: Lion Brand Heartland, 251 yd (230 m), 5 oz (142 g), 100% acrylic: 1 ball 136-138T Lassen Volcanic

Hook
US Size G/6 (4 mm) crochet hook. Adjust hook size if necessary to work tightly.

Gauge
Exact gauge is not critical for this piece. Work tightly to ensure stuffing does not show through.

Notions
Yarn needle
Polyester stuffing
Black embroidery thread
1 pair 6 mm black safety eyes
Scissors
Stitch marker
Card stock
Hot glue or double-sided tape

Body

Make a magic loop.

Rnd 1: Work 6 sc in loop; do not join, work in continuous rnds—6 sc.

Place marker in last sc made to indicate end of rnd. Move marker up as each rnd is completed.

Rnd 2: Work 2 sc in each st around—12 sc.

Rnd 3: [2 sc in next st, sc in next st] around—18 sc.

Rnd 4: [Sc in next st, 2 sc in next st, sc in next st] around—24 sc.

Rnd 5: [2 sc in next st, sc in next 3 sts] around—30 sc.

Rnd 6: [Sc in next 2 sts, 2 sc in next st, sc in next 2 sts] around—36 sc.

Rnd 7: [2 sc in next st, sc in next 5 sts] around—42 sc.

Rnd 8: [Sc in next 3 sts, 2 sc in next st, sc in next 3 sts] around—48 sc.

Rnds 9–14: Sc in each st around.

Rnd 15: [Sc in next 5 sts, inv-dec, sc in next 5 sts] 4 times—44 sc.

Rnds 16 and 17: Sc in each st around.

Rnd 18: [Inv-dec, sc in next 9 sts] 4 times—40 sc.

Rnds 19 and 20: Sc in each st around.

Rnd 21: [Sc in next st, ch 4, sk next 4 sts] 8 times (tentacle openings made); join with sl st in first sc—8 sc and 8 ch-4 sps.

Rnd 22: Sc in each st and ch around—40 sc.

Rnd 23: [Sc in next 4 sts, inv-dec, sc in next 4 sts] 4 times—36 sc.

Rnd 24: [Sc in next 2 sts, inv-dec, sc in next 2 sts] around—30 sc.

Add safety eyes between Rnds 16 and 17, about 6 sts apart.

Stuff Body and continue stuffing as work progresses.

Rnd 25: [Inv-dec, sc in next 3 sts] around—24 sc.

Rnd 26: [Sc in next st, inv-dec, sc in next st] around—18 sc.

Rnd 27: [Inv-dec, sc in next st] around—12 sc.

Rnd 28: Inv-dec around—6 sc.

Fasten off, leaving a long tail. Sew remaining 6 sts closed.

Tentacle (Make 8)

Draw up a loop in first skipped st of any tentacle opening in Rnd 20.

Rnd 1: Beg in same st as joining, sc in 4 skipped sts, sc in underside of next 4 ch; do not join, work in continuous rnds—8 sc.

Place marker in last sc made to indicate end of rnd. Move marker up as each rnd is completed.

Rnds 2–11: Sc in each st around.

Stuff Tentacle and continue stuffing as work progresses.

Rnd 12: Inv-dec, sc in each st around—7 sc.

Rnd 13: Sc in each st around.

Rnd 14: Inv-dec, sc in each st around—6 sc.

Rnds 15–18: Rep Rnds 13 and 14 twice—4 sc in Rnd 18.

Rnd 19: Sc in each st around.

Fasten off, leaving a long tail for sewing. Sew remaining 4 sts closed.

Finishing

Using black embroidery thread, embroider a smile in a V shape between the eyes.

Write or print an inspirational message on card stock and cut to desired size. Use hot glue or double-sided tape to attach sign to a tentacle or two.

Weave in ends.

You're the stuff
of legends.

DRAGON

This dragon may be small but wants to fiercely remind you that you are amazing! Like him, you are flying high, soaring through your challenges with grace, and landing exactly where you need to be right now. And above everything else, you are absolutely magical.

AFFIRMATIONS for THE DRAGON

You're the stuff of legends.

Don't let anyone dull your flame.

You're able to scale any heights.

I'm not blowing smoke—you're the best!

If you're dragon, I'll be there to pick you up.

Measurements
5" (12.7 cm) × 6" (15.2 cm)

Yarn
Worsted weight (#4 medium)

Shown here: Lion Brand Heartland, 251 yd (230 m), 5 oz (142 g), 100% acrylic: 1 ball 136-134V Gateway Arch (A)

Lion Brand Basic Stitch Anti Pilling,185 yd (170 m), 3½ oz (100 g), 100% acrylic: 1 ball 202-110AW Stonewash (B)

Hook
US Size G/6 (4 mm) crochet hook. Adjust hook size if necessary to work tightly.

Gauge
Exact gauge is not critical for this piece. Work tightly to ensure stuffing does not show through.

Notions
Yarn needle
Polyester stuffing
1 pair 6 mm black safety eyes
Scissors
Stitch marker
Card stock
Black embroidery floss

Feet (Make 4)

With A, make a magic loop.

Rnd 1: Work 6 sc in loop, join with sl st in first sc—6 sc.

Rnd 2: Ch 1, working in BLO sc in each st around, join with sl st in first sc.

Rnd 3: Ch 1, sc in each st around, join with sl st in first sc.

Fasten off, stuff. Set Feet aside to join to Body.

Body

With A, ch 5.

Rnd 1: Sc in 2nd ch from hook, sc in next 2 ch, 3 sc in last ch; working along opposite side of foundation ch, sc in next 3 ch, 3 sc in last ch (ch that was skipped at beg of rnd); join with sl st in first sc—12 sc.

Rnd 2: Ch 1, [sc in next 3 sts, 2 sc in each of next 3 sts] 2 times; join with sl st in first sc—18 sc.

Rnd 3 (Join Feet): Ch 1, sc in next 3 sts, sc in the 6 sts of first Foot, sc in next 6 sts of Rnd 2, sc in the 6 sts of 2nd Foot, sc in next 3 sts of Rnd 2, sc in the 6 sts of 3rd Foot, sc in next 6 sts of Rnd 2, sc in the 6 sts of 4th Foot; join with sl st in first sc—42 sc.

Rnds 4–8: Ch 1, sc in each st around; join with sl st in first sc.

Rnd 9: Ch 1, sc in next 20 sts, ch 6, sk next 6 sts (tail opening made), sc in last 16 sts; join with sl st in first sc—36 sc, 1 ch-6 sp.

Rnd 10: Ch 1, [sc in next 5 sts, sc2tog] around; join with sl st in first sc—36 sc.

Rnd 11: Ch 1, sc in each st around; join with sl st in first sc.

Place marker in last sc made to indicate end of rnd. Move marker up as each rnd is completed.

Rnd 12 (Neck): Sc in next 9 sts, sk next 24 sts, sc in next 3 sts—12 sc.

Rnds 13: Sc in each st around.

Rnd 14: [Inv-dec, sc in next 2 sts] around—9 sc.

Rnd 15: Sc in next st, 2 sc in each of next 3 sts, sc in next 5 sts—12 sc.

Rnd 16: Sc in next st, [2 sc in next st, sc in next st] 3 times, sc in next 5 sts—15 sc.

Rnd 17: Sc in next st, [sc in next st, 2 sc in next st, sc in next st] 3 times, sc in next 5 sts—18 sc.

Rnd 18: Sc in next st, [2 sc in next st, sc in next 3 sts] 3 times, sc in next 5 sts—21 sc.

Rnds 19 and 20: Sc in each st around.

Rnd 21: Sc in next 6 sts, [inv-dec] 3 times, sc in next 9 sts—18 sc.

Add safety eyes between Rnds 19 and 20 on either side of head.

Stuff Body and continue stuffing as work progresses.

Rnd 22: [Inv-dec, sc in next st] around—12 sc.

Rnd 23: Inv-dec around—6 sc.

Fasten off, leaving a long tail for sewing. Sew remaining 6 sts closed.

Muzzle

With A, make a magic loop.

Rnd 1: Work 6 sc in loop; do not join. Work in continuous rnds—6 sc.

Place marker in last sc made to indicate end of rnd. Move marker up as each rnd is completed.

Rnd 2: [2 sc in next st, sc in next st] around—9 sc.

Rnds 3 and 4: Sc in each st around.

Fasten off, leaving a long tail for sewing.

Tail

Draw up a loop of A in first skipped sc of Rnd 8 of Body.

Rnd 1: Ch 1, sc in same st as joining, sc in next 4 sts, sc2tog over next sc and gap before ch-6 space, sc in underside of next 5 ch, sc2tog over next ch and gap before first sc; do not join, work in continuous rnds—12 sc.

Place a marker in last sc made to indicate end of rnd. Move marker up as each rnd is completed.

Rnds 2–4: Sc in each st around.

Rnd 5: [Inv-dec, sc in next 2 sts] around—9 sc.

Rnds 6–8: Sc in each st around.

Rnd 9: Inv-dec, sc in each st around—8 sc.

Rnds 10 and 11: Sc in each st around.

Rnd 12: Inv-dec, sc in each st around—7 sc.

Rnds 13–15: Rep Rnds 10–12—6 sc in Rnd 15.

Stuff Tail and continue stuffing as work progresses.

Rnds 16–21: Rep Rnds 10–12 twice—4 sc in Rnd 21.

Rnds 22 and 23: Sc in each st around.

Fasten off, leaving a long tail for sewing. Sew remaining 4 sts closed.

Horn (Make 2)

With B, make a magic loop.

Rnd 1: Work 3 sc in loop; do not join. Work in continuous rnds—3 sc.

Place marker in last sc made to indicate end of rnd. Move marker up as each rnd is completed.

Rnd 2: 2 sc in next st, sc in next 2 sts—4 sc.

Rnds 3–5: Sc in each st around.

Fasten off, leaving a long tail for sewing.

Ear (Make 2)

With A, make a magic loop.

Rnd 1: Work 4 sc in loop, do not join—4 sc.

Fasten off, leaving a long tail for sewing.

Spikes

With B, ch 3.

Row 1: Sc in 2nd ch from hook, dc in next ch (one spike made), [ch 4, sc in 2nd ch from hook, dc in next ch, sk next ch] 10 times—11 spikes.

Fasten off, leaving a long tail for sewing.

Wing (Make 2)

With A, ch 10.

Row 1: Sc in 2nd ch from hook and in next 2 ch, hdc in next 3 ch, dc in last 3 ch, turn—9 sts.

Row 2: Ch 3 (counts as first dc), working in BLO, dc in next 2 sts, hdc in next 3 sts, sc in last 3 sts, turn.

Row 3: Ch 1, working in BLO, sc in next 3 sts, hdc in next 3 sts, dc in last 3 sts, turn.

Rows 4–7: Rep Rows 2 and 3.

Row 8: Rep Row 2, do not turn.

Row 9: Ch 1, work 7 sc evenly spaced in ends of rows along side edge—7 sc.

Fasten off, leaving a long tail for sewing.

Finishing

Using a length of A, sew back seam closed.

Using a length of A, sew small gap at top of each Foot closed.

Stuff Muzzle and sew to front of head.

Using a length of B, embroider 2 lines for nostrils on either side of Muzzle.

Sew Horns to top of head.

Sew Spikes along spine of Dragon, from top of head to tip of tail.

Sew Ears to top of head on either side of Horns.

Sew Wings to either side of Body.

Write or print an inspirational message on card stock and cut to desired size. Cut a short length of embroidery floss. Poke holes in top two corners of sign and draw end of thread through. Tie knots to secure. Hang sign from Dragon's nose.

Weave in ends.

SLOTH

A lot of wonderful things can happen with time and intention. This adorable little sloth is here to remind you that it's okay to take your time and do your best. Everyone moves through life at their own pace, and when things get overwhelming, it's okay to slow down and enjoy the little things.

AFFIRMATIONS for THE SLOTH

Take your time!

Hang in there!

Slow down and enjoy the journey.

You are claw-some.

Measurements
5" (12.7 cm) × 2½" (6.4 cm), sitting

Yarn
Worsted weight (#4 medium)

Shown here: Lion Brand Basic Stitch Anti Pilling, 185 yd (170 m), 3½ oz (100 g), 100% acrylic: 1 ball each 202-100 White (A), 202-122T Hazelnut (B), 202-125AA Truffle (C), and 202-153 Black (D)

Hook
US Size G/6 (4 mm) crochet hook. Adjust hook size if necessary to work tightly.

Gauge
Exact gauge is not critical for this piece. Work tightly to ensure stuffing does not show through.

Notions
Yarn needle
Polyester stuffing
1 pair 9 mm black safety eyes
Scissors
Stitch marker
Card stock
Hot glue or double-sided tape

Take your
time!

Claw (Make 4)

With A, ch 5.

Row 1: Sl st in 2nd ch from hook, sl st in next 3 ch (first digit made), [ch 6, sl st in 2nd ch from hook, sl st in next 3 ch, sk last ch of the ch-6] 2 times—3 digits for 1 claw.

Fasten off.

Limb (Make 4)

With B, make a magic loop.

Rnd 1: Work 6 sc in loop; do not join. Work in continuous rnds—6 sc.

Place marker in last sc made to indicate end of rnd. Move marker up as each rnd is completed.

Rnd 2: Sc in each st around.

Insert a Claw from inside (WS) pulling each of the 3 digits through a stitch between Rnds 1 and 2. Secure tails of Claw inside the Limb by tying a knot with the starting and finishing ends.

Rnds 3–12: Sc in each st around.

Fasten off.

Body

With B, beg at bottom of piece, make a magic loop.

Rnd 1: Work 6 sc in loop; do not join. Work in continuous rnds—6 sc.

Place marker in last sc made to indicate end of rnd. Move marker up as each rnd is completed.

Rnd 2: Work 2 sc in each st around—12 sc.

Rnd 3: Sc in next 6 sts, sc in each st of first Limb, sc in next 6 sts, sc in each st of 2nd Limb—24 sc.

Rnd 4: [2 sc in next st, sc in next 3 sts] around—30 sc.

Rnds 5–9: Sc in each st around.

Rnd 10: [Inv-dec, sc in next 3 sts] around—24 sc.

Rnds 11 and 12: Sc in each st around.

Rnd 13: Sc in next 11 sts, sc in each st of 3rd Limb, sc in next 12 sts, sc in each st of 4th Limb, sc in last st—36 sc.

Rnd 14: [Sc in next 2 sts, inv-dec, sc in next 2 sts] around—30 sc.

Rnd 15: [Inv-dec, sc in next 3 sts] around—24 sc.

Rnd 16: [Sc in next st, inv-dec, sc in next st] around—18 sc.

Rnd 17: [Inv-dec, sc in next st] around—12 sc.

Fasten off. Stuff Body.

Eyes (Make 2)

With C, ch 9.

Row 1: Sl st in 2nd ch from hook, sl st in next 2 ch, sc in next 4 ch, 3 sc in last ch; working along opposite side of foundation ch, sc in next 4 ch, sl st in last 4 ch (last sl st is worked in skipped ch at beg of row)—18 sts.

Fasten off, leaving a long tail for sewing. Insert safety eyes in increase end of Eyes, but do not secure the backing.

Head

Draw up a loop of A, anywhere in neck edge of Body.

Rnd 1: Work 3 sc in each st around; do not join, work in continuous rnds—36 sc.

Place marker in last sc made to indicate end of rnd. Move marker up as each rnd is completed.

Rnds 2–9: Sc in each st around.

Rnd 10: [Sc in next 2 sts, inv-dec, sc in next 2 sts] around—30 sc.

Use safety eyes to add Eyes between Rnds 7 and 8, with Eye pieces on an angle slanting downward toward neck. Using tails, sew Eyes to Head.

Rnd 11: [Inv-dec, sc in next 3 sts] around—24 sc.

Stuff Head and continue stuffing as work progresses.

Rnd 12: [Sc in next st, inv-dec, sc in next st] around—18 sc.

Rnd 13: [Inv-dec, sc in next st] around—12 sc.

Rnd 14: Inv-dec around—6 sc.

Fasten off, leaving a tail for sewing. Sew remaining 6 sts closed.

Nose

With D, ch 2.

Row 1: Work 2 sc in 2nd ch from hook, turn—2 sc.

Row 2: Ch 1, 2 sc in each sc—4 sc.

Fasten off, leaving a long tail for sewing.

Head Cap

With B, make a magic loop.

Rnd 1: Work 6 sc in loop; do not join. Work in continuous rnds—6 sc.

Place marker in last sc made to indicate end of rnd. Move marker up as each rnd is completed.

Rnd 2: Work 2 sc in each st around—12 sc.

Rnd 3: [2 sc in next st, sc in next st] around—18 sc.

Rnd 4: [Sc in next st, 2 sc in next st, sc in next st] around—24 sc.

Rnd 5: [2 sc in next st, sc in next 3 sts] around—30 sc.

Rnd 6: [Sc in next 2 sts, 2 sc in next st, sc in next 2 sts] around—36 sc.

Rnds 7–11: Sc in each st around.

Fasten off, leaving a long tail for sewing.

Finishing

Sew Nose to center of Head between Eyes.

Sew Cap to top of Head with bottom of Cap touching the neckline. Cap should overlap the bottom edges of Eyes.

Write or print an inspirational message on card stock and cut to desired size. Use hot glue or double-sided tape to attach sign to hands.

Weave in ends.

Best Friend

PUPPY

This little pup is the ultimate cheerleader. You went for a little self-care walk today? That's amazing! You got a few things done and then took a nap? Incredible! Life can be "ruff," but remember that happiness can be found in the smallest moments.

AFFIRMATIONS for THE PUPPY

Best Friend

Life would be "ruff" without you!

You're top dog.

Life's a walk in the park with you around.

Doggone it, you're awesome!

Measurements
4½" (11.4 cm) × 2" (5.1 cm)

Yarn
Worsted weight (#4 medium)

Shown here: Lion Brand Basic Stitch Anti Pilling, 185 yd (170 m), 3½ oz (100 g), 100% acrylic: 1 ball each 202-134U Honey (A) and 202-122T Hazelnut (B)

Hook
US Size G/6 (4 mm) crochet hook. Adjust hook size if necessary to work tightly.

Gauge
Exact gauge is not critical for this piece. Work tightly to ensure stuffing does not show through.

Notions
Yarn needle
Polyester stuffing
Orange embroidery thread
Black embroidery thread
1 pair 6 mm black safety eyes
Scissors
Stitch marker
Card stock
Hot glue or double-sided tape

Front Legs (Make 2)

With A, make a magic loop.

Rnd 1: Work 6 sc in loop; join with sl st in first sc—6 sc.

Rnd 2: Ch 1, 2 sc in each of next 3 sts (for front of foot), sc in next 3 sts; join with sl st in first sc—9 sc.

Rnd 3: Ch 1, sc in each st around; join with sl st in first sc.

Rnd 4: Ch 1, [inv-dec] 3 times, sc in next 3 sts; join with sl st in first sc—6 sc.

Stuff Front Leg and continue stuffing as work progresses.

Fasten off. Draw up a loop of B in back of foot.

Rnd 5: Ch 1, sl st in each st around; join with sl st in first sl st—6 sl sts.

Rnd 6: Ch 1, working in BLO, sc around; join with sl st in first sc.

Rnds 7–10: Ch 1, sc around; join with sl st in first sc.

Fasten off.

Body

With B, make a magic loop.

Rnd 1: Work 6 sc in loop; do not join. Work in continuous rnds—6 sc.

Place marker in last sc made to indicate end of rnd. Move marker up as each rnd is completed.

Rnd 2: Work 2 sc in each st around—12 sc.

Rnd 3: [2 sc in next st, sc in next st] around—18 sc.

Rnd 4: [Sc in next st, 2 sc in next st, sc in next st] around—24 sc.

Rnds 5–10: Sc in each st around.

Rnd 11 (Join Front Legs): Sc in next 3 sts; beg at back of first Front Leg, sc in each st of Leg, sc in next 3 sts of Rnd 10; beg at back of 2nd Front Leg, sc in each st of Leg, sc in next 18 sts of Rnd 10—36 sc.

Rnds 12 and 13: Sc in each st around.

Rnd 14: Inv-dec, sc in next 19 sts, [inv-dec, sc in next st] 5 times—30 sc.

Rnds 15 and 16: Sc in each st around.

Rnd 17: [Inv-dec, sc in next 3 sts] around—24 sc.

Rnd 18: [Sc in next st, inv-dec, sc in next st] around—18 sc.

Stuff Body and continue stuffing as work progresses.

Rnd 19: [Inv-dec, sc in next st] around—12 sc.

Do not fasten off. Continue to Head.

Head

Rnd 1: Continuing with B, 3 sc in each st around—36 sc.

Rnds 2–7: Sc in each st around.

Rnd 8: [Sc in next st, inv-dec, sc in next st] around—27 sc.

Rnd 9: [Inv-dec, sc in next 7 sts] around—24 sc.

Rnds 10 and 11: Sc in each st around.

Add safety eyes between Rnds 8 and 9, about 4 sts apart. Stuff Head and continue stuffing as work progresses.

Rnd 12: [Sc in next st, inv-dec, sc in next st] around—18 sc.

Rnd 13: [Inv-dec, sc in next st] around—12 sc.

Rnd 14: Inv-dec around—6 sc.

Fasten off, leaving a long tail for sewing. Sew remaining 6 sts closed.

Back Legs (Make 2)

With A, make a magic loop.

Rnds 1–6: Work same as Rnds 1–6 of Front Legs—6 sc.

Rnd 7: Ch 1, [2 sc in next st, sc in next st] around; join with sl st in first sc—9 sc.

Rnd 8: Ch 1, sc in each st around; join with sl st in first sc.

Stuff Back Leg and continue stuffing as work progresses.

Rnd 9: Ch 1, [inv-dec, sc in next st] 3 times; join with sl st in first sc—6 sc.

Fasten off, leaving a long tail for sewing.

Ears (Make 2)

With A, make a magic loop.

Rnd 1: Work 6 sc in loop; do not join. Work in continuous rnds—6 sc.

Place marker in last sc made to indicate end of rnd. Move marker up as each rnd is completed.

Rnd 2: [2 sc in next st, sc in next st] around—9 sc.

Rnds 3–5: Sc in each st.

Rnd 6: Sl st in next st, ch 1, pinch top of piece, matching sts along each side of top edge; working through both thicknesses, sc in next 4 sts to close top of Ear.

Fasten off, leaving a long tail for sewing.

Muzzle

With A, make a magic loop.

Rnd 1: Work 6 sc in loop; do not join. Work in continuous rnds—6 sc.

Place marker in last sc made to indicate end of rnd. Move marker up as each rnd is completed.

Rnd 2: Work 2 sc in each st around—12 sc.

Rnd 3: Sc in each st around.

Fasten off, leaving a long tail for sewing.

Tail

With B, make a magic loop.

Rnd 1: Work 3 sc in loop; do not join. Work in continuous rnds—3 sc.

Place marker in last sc made to indicate end of rnd. Move marker up as each rnd is completed.

Rnds 2–4: Work 2 sc in first st, sc in each st around—6 sc in Rnd 4.

Rnds 5 and 6: Sc in each st around.

Rnds 7 and 8: Inv-dec, sc in each st around—4 sc in Rnd 8.

Fasten off, leaving a long tail for sewing.

Finishing

Sew Back Legs to either side of Body.

Sew Ears to top of Head.

Sew Tail to back of Body.

Using black embroidery thread, embroider a triangle nose on Muzzle.

Sew Muzzle to front of Head under eyes.

Tie a length of orange embroidery thread around Puppy's neck for collar.

Write or print an inspirational message on card stock and cut to desired size. Use hot glue or double-sided tape to attach sign to Puppy.

Weave in ends.

LION

Look at you! Just like this darling lion, you are determined, persistent, resilient, and oh-so powerful! We see you taking pride in your achievements. Keep it up and carry around this handsome feline as a constant reminder that you can do it with mane-character energy!

AFFIRMATIONS for THE LION

I ain't lion, you're the best!

Life's a jungle,
but you're the king.

Be the mane character
of your story.

Feline good!

You're a roaring success.

Measurements
6" (15.2 cm) × 3½" (8.9 cm)

Yarn
Worsted weight (#4 medium)

Shown here: Lion Brand Heartland, 251 yd (230 m), 5 oz (142 g), 100% acrylic: 1 ball each 136-098U Acadia (A) and 136-126U Sequoia (C)

Lion Brand Basic Stitch Anti Pilling, 185 yd (170 m), 3½ oz (100 g), 100% acrylic: 1 ball 202-134U Honey (B)

Hook
US Size G/6 (4 mm) crochet hook. Adjust hook size if necessary to work tightly.

Gauge
Exact gauge is not critical for this piece. Work tightly to ensure stuffing does not show through.

Notions
Yarn needle
Polyester stuffing
Black embroidery thread
White embroidery thread
1 pair 6 mm black safety eyes
Scissors
Stitch marker
Card stock
Hot glue or double-sided tape

I ain't lion,
you're the best!

Front Legs (Make 2)

With A, make a magic loop.

Rnd 1: Work 6 sc in loop; join with sl st in first sc—6 sc.

Rnd 2: Ch 1, 2 sc in each of next 3 sts (for front of foot), sc in next 3 sts; join with sl st in first sc—9 sc.

Rnd 3: Ch 1 sc in each st around; join with sl st in first sc.

Stuff Front Leg and continue stuffing as work progresses.

Fasten off. Change to B, drawing up a loop of B in back of foot.

Rnd 4: Ch 1, [inv-dec] 3 times, sc in next 3 sts; join with sl st in first sc—6 sc.

Rnds 5–9: Ch 1, sc in each st around; join with sl st in first sc.

Fasten off.

Body

With B, make a magic loop.

Rnd 1: Work 6 sc in loop; do not join. Work in continuous rnds—6 sc.

Place marker in last sc made to indicate end of rnd. Move marker up as each rnd is completed.

Rnd 2: Work 2 sc in each st around—12 sc.

Rnd 3: [2 sc in next st, sc in next st] around—18 sc.

Rnd 4: [Sc in next st, 2 sc in next st, sc in next st] around—24 sc.

Rnds 5–10: Sc in each st around.

Rnd 11 (Join Front Legs): Sc in next 3 sts; beg at back of first Front Leg, sc in each st of Leg, sc in next 3 sts of Rnd 10; beg at back of 2nd Front Leg, sc in each st of Leg, sc in next 18 sts of Rnd 10—36 sc.

Rnds 12 and 13: Sc in each st around.

Rnd 14: Inv-dec, sc in next 19 sts, [inv-dec, sc in next st] 5 times—30 sc.

Rnds 15 and 16: Sc in each st around.

Rnd 17: [Inv-dec, sc in next 3 sts] around—24 sc.

Rnd 18: [Sc in next st, inv-dec, sc in next st] around—18 sc.

Stuff Body and continue stuffing as work progresses.

Rnd 19: [Inv-dec, sc in next st] around—12 sc.

Do not fasten off. Continue to Head.

Head

Rnd 1: Continuing with B, 3 sc in each st around—36 sc.

Rnds 2–7: Sc in each st around.

Rnd 8: [Sc in next st, inv-dec, sc in next st] around—27 sc.

Rnd 9: [Inv-dec, sc in next 7 sts] around—24 sc.

Rnds 10 and 11: Sc in each st around.

Add safety eyes between Rnds 8 and 9, about 4 sts apart. Stuff Head and continue stuffing as work progresses.

Rnd 12: [Sc in next st, inv-dec, sc in next st] around—18 sc.

Rnd 13: [Inv-dec, sc in next st] around—12 sc.

Rnd 14: Inv-dec around—6 sc.

Fasten off, leaving a long tail for sewing. Sew remaining 6 sts closed.

Back Legs (Make 2)

With A, make a magic loop.

Rnds 1–5: Work same as Rnds 1–5 of Front Legs—6 sc.

Rnd 6: [2 sc in next st, sc in next st] around—9 sc.

Rnds 7 and 8: Sc in each st around.

Stuff Back Leg and continue stuffing as work progresses.

Rnd 9: [Inv-dec, sc in next st] 3 times—6 sc.

Fasten off, leaving a long tail for sewing.

Ears (Make 2)

With B, make a magic loop.

Rnd 1: Work 6 sc in loop; do not join. Work in continuous rnds—6 sc.

Fasten off, leaving a long tail for sewing.

Muzzle

With A, make a magic loop.

Rnd 1: Work 6 sc in loop; do not join. Work in continuous rnds—6 sc.

Place marker in last sc made to indicate end of rnd. Move marker up as each rnd is completed.

Rnd 2: Work 2 sc in each st around—12 sc.

Rnd 3: Sc in each st around.

Fasten off, leaving a long tail for sewing.

Tail

With B, ch 11.

Row 1: Sc in 2nd ch from hook and in each across—10 sc.

Fasten off, leaving a long tail for sewing. Using several lengths of C, add fringe to end of Tail.

Mane

With C, ch 37.

Row 1: Sc in 2nd ch from hook and in each across, turn—36 sc.

Row 2: [Ch 10, sl st in next sc of Row 1] across.

Fasten off, leaving a long tail for sewing.

Finishing

Sew Back Legs to either side of Body.

Sew Tail to back of body.

Using black embroidery thread, embroider a triangle nose on Muzzle.

Using white embroidery thread, embroider a "fleck" on nose.

Sew Muzzle to front of Head under eyes.

Sew Mane around face overlapping beginning and end of Mane underneath the chin.

Sew Ears to top of Head overlapping Mane.

Write or print an inspirational message on card stock and cut to desired size. Use hot glue or double-sided tape to attach sign to Lion.

Weave in ends.

You're
all heart.
You're
so good it's
spooky.
You run rings around
the competition.
You're a
really fungi.

CHAPTER 4

A UNIVERSE OF POSITIVITY

In this chapter, we explore a world of amigurumi creations that bring comfort, joy, and positivity. From colorful crayons and rainbows to otherworldly planets and ghosts to friendly acorns and mushrooms, each adorable amigurumi will warm your heart, spark creativity, and remind you of the simple joys in life.

Stay sharp!

CACTUS

It's truly amazing how some of us can thrive in difficult environments. And not only thrive, but blossom into something absolutely beautiful! Self-protected, self-nurtured, and growing in place despite all of the odds stacked against you, you are truly a marvel!

AFFIRMATIONS for THE CACTUS

Stay sharp!

You thrive no matter the conditions.

You're always on point.

Bloom where you're planted.

Looking sharp!

Measurements
5" (12.7 cm) × 3" (7.6 cm)

Yarn
Worsted weight (#4 medium)

Shown here: Lion Brand Basic Stitch Anti Pilling, 185 yd (170 m), 3½ oz (100 g), 100% acrylic: 1 ball each 202-122T Hazelnut (A) and 202-125AA Truffle (B)

Lion Brand Vanna's Choice, 170 yd (156 m), 3½ oz (100 g), 100% acrylic: 1 ball each 860-172C Kelly Green (C) and 860-113 Scarlet (D)

Hook
US Size G/6 (4 mm) crochet hook. Adjust hook size if necessary to work tightly.

Gauge
Exact gauge is not critical for this piece. Work tightly to ensure stuffing does not show through.

Notions
Yarn needle
Polyester stuffing
Black embroidery thread
Black craft wire
1 pair 6 mm black safety eyes
Scissors
Stitch marker
Card stock
Hot glue or double-sided tape

Pot

With A, make a magic loop.

Rnd 1: Work 6 sc in loop; do not join. Work in continuous rnds—6 sc.

Place marker in last sc made to indicate end of rnd. Move marker up as each rnd is completed.

Rnd 2: Work 2 sc in each st around—12 sc.

Rnd 3: [2 sc in next st, sc in next st] around—18 sc.

Rnd 4: [Sc in next st, 2 sc in next st, sc in next st] around—24 sc.

Rnd 5: [2 sc in next st, sc in next 3 sts] around—30 sc.

Rnds 6 and 7: Working in BLO, sl st in each st around—30 sl sts.

Rnd 8: Working in BLO, sc in each st around.

Rnds 9 and 10: Sc in each st around.

Rnd 11: [2 sc in next st, sc in next 9 sts] around—33 sc.

Rnd 12: Sc in each st around.

Rnd 13: [Sc in next 5 sts, 2 sc in next st, sc in next 5 sts] around—36 sc.

Rnd 14: Sc in each st around.

Rnd 15: Working in BLO, sc in each st around.

Rnd 16: Hdc in each free FLO of Rnd 14—36 hdc.

Rnd 17: Working in BLO, sl st in each st around—36 sl sts.

Fasten off. Add safety eyes between Rnds 10 and 11, about 4 sts apart.

Stuff Pot.

Soil

With B, make a magic loop.

Rnds 1–5: Work same as Rnds 1–5 of Pot—30 sc.

Rnd 6: [Sc in next 2 sts, 2 sc in next st, sc in next 2 sts] around—36 sc.

Fasten off, leaving a long tail for sewing.

Cactus

With C, ch 16.

Row 1: Sl st in 2nd ch from hook and in next 4 ch, sc in next 5 ch, sl st in last 5 ch, turn—15 sts.

Rows 2–30: Ch 1, working in BLO, sl st in first 5 sts, sc in next 5 sts, sl st in last 5 sts, turn.

Fasten off, leaving a long tail for sewing.

Flower

With D, make a magic loop.

Rnd 1: [Sc in loop, ch 9] 9 times; join with sl st in first sc—9 sc.

Fasten off, leaving a long tail for sewing.

Finishing

Sew first row of Cactus to last row, making a tube. Sew one end of tube closed and weave in end. Stuff Cactus.

Using a length of C, sew open end of Cactus to top of Soil.

Sew Soil to top of Pot.

Sew Flower to top of Cactus.

Cut a piece of black craft wire about 2½ to 3 times as long as the width of the piece. Gently poke the wire through center of piece at arm level, leaving equal-length ends sticking out of sides for arms.

Using black embroidery thread, embroider a smile in a V shape below the eyes.

Write or print an inspirational message on card stock and cut to desired size. Use hot glue or double-sided tape to attach sign to hands.

Weave in ends.

PLANET

If you've been feeling a little bit lost in space, fear not! This sweet little planet with its cute smile is here to cheer you up! It's star-struck by how awesome you are and wanted us to tell you it thinks you're out of this world!

AFFIRMATIONS for THE PLANET

It's okay to take up space.

You're out of this world!

You run rings around the competition.

I'd be lost in space without you.

Measurements
2½" (6.4 cm) × 4" (10.2 cm)

Yarn
Worsted weight (#4 medium)

Shown here: WeCrochet Brava Worsted 218 yd (200 m), 3½ oz (100 g), 100% acrylic: 1 ball 28422 Corn Flower (A)

WeCrochet Brava Speckle 218 yd (200 m), 3½ oz (100 g), 100% acrylic: 1 ball 29242 Cake Pop Speckle (B)

Hook
US Size G/6 (4 mm) crochet hook. Adjust hook size if necessary to work tightly.

Gauge
Exact gauge is not critical for this piece. Work tightly to ensure stuffing does not show through.

Notions
Yarn needle
Polyester stuffing
Black embroidery thread
Black craft wire
1 pair 6 mm black safety eyes
Scissors
Stitch marker
Card stock
Hot glue or double-sided tape

Special Stitch
Bpsc (back post single crochet) = Insert hook from back to front then to back again around post of next st, yarn over and draw up a loop, yarn over and draw through 2 loops.

It's okay to
take up space.

Body

With A, ch 2.

Rnd 1: Work 6 sc in 2nd ch from hook; do not join, work in continuous rnds—6 sc.

Place a marker in last sc made to indicate end of rnd. Move marker up as each rnd is completed.

Rnd 2: Work 2 sc in each st around—12 sc.

Rnd 3: [2 sc in next st, sc in next st] around—18 sc.

Rnd 4: [Sc in next st, 2 sc in next st, sc in next st] around—24 sc.

Rnd 5: [2 sc in next st, sc in next 3 sts] around—30 sc.

Rnd 6: [Sc in next 2 sts, 2 sc in next st, sc in next 2 sts] around—36 sc.

Rnd 7: [2 sc in next st, sc in next 5 sts] around—42 sc.

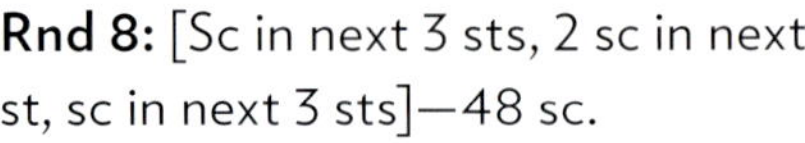

Rnd 8: [Sc in next 3 sts, 2 sc in next st, sc in next 3 sts]—48 sc.

Rnds 9–12: Sc in each st around.

Rnd 13: Sl st in next st, ch 1, Bpsc in each st around—48 Bpsc.

Rnds 14–16: Sc in each st around.

Rnd 17: [Sc in next 3 sts, inv-dec, sc in next 3 sts] around—42 sc.

Rnd 18: [Inv-dec, sc in next 5 sts] around—36 sc.

Rnd 19: [Sc in next 2 sts, inv-dec, sc in next 2 sts] around—30 sc.

Add safety eyes between Rnds 9 and 10, about 3 sts apart.

Stuff Body and continue stuffing as work progresses.

Rnd 20: [Inv-dec, sc in next 3 sts] around—24 sc.

Rnd 21: [Sc in next st, inv-dec, sc in next st] around—18 sc.

Rnd 22: [Inv-dec, sc in next st] around—12 sc.

Rnd 23: Inv-dec around—6 sc.

Fasten off, leaving a tail for sewing. Sew remaining 6 sts closed.

Planetary Ring

Join B to any st of Rnd 12 of Body.

Rnd 1: Ch 1, [2 sc in next st, sc in next 7 sts] around; do not join, work in continuous rnds—54 sc.

Place a marker in last sc made to indicate end of rnd. Move marker up as each rnd is completed.

Rnd 2: [Sc in next 4 sts, 2 sc in next st, sc in next 4 sts] around—60 sc.

Rnd 3: [2 sc in next st, sc in next 9 sts] around—66 sc.

Rnd 4: [Sc in next 5 sts, 2 sc, sc in next 5 sts] around—72 sc.

Fasten off.

Legs (Make 1)

With A, ch 20.

Fasten off and trim ends.

Finishing

Cut a piece of black craft wire about 2½ to 3 times as long as the width of the piece. Gently poke the wire through center of piece at arm level, leaving equal-length ends sticking out of sides for arms.

Thread Legs through bottom of Body, leaving equal-length ends of ch-20 hanging down for legs. With a length of A, sew a few stitches to secure Legs.

Using black embroidery thread, embroider a smile in a V shape below the eyes.

Write or print an inspirational message on card stock and cut to desired size. Use hot glue or double-sided tape to attach sign to hands.

Weave in ends.

I have so
mushroom in
my heart for you.

MUSHROOM

We think you're as cute as a button, no cap! Our crocheted fungus doesn't leave mush-room for any more adorableness, and even if you don't like to eat mushrooms yourself, we think this little guy will grow on you!

AFFIRMATIONS for THE MUSHROOM

I have so mushroom in my heart for you.

You're a really fungi.

You handled today spore-tacularly!

I love you very mush.

Need some morel support?

Measurements
3½" (8.9 cm) × 2½" (6.4 cm)

Yarn
Worsted weight (#4 medium)

Shown here: Lion Brand Vanna's Choice, 170 yd (156 m), 3½ oz (100 g), 100% acrylic: 1 ball each 860-113 Scarlet (A), and 860-100 White (C)

Loops & Threads Impeccable, 277 yd (253 m), 4.5 oz (127.5 g), 100% acrylic: 1 ball 75 Heather (B)

Hook
US Size G/6 (4 mm) crochet hook. Adjust hook size if necessary to work tightly.

Gauge
Exact gauge is not critical for this piece. Work tightly to ensure stuffing does not show through.

Notions
Yarn needle
Polyester stuffing
Black embroidery thread
Black craft wire
1 pair 6 mm black safety eyes
White felt
Scissors
Stitch marker
Card stock
Hot glue or double-sided tape

Cap

With A, ch 2.

Rnd 1: Work 6 sc in 2nd ch from hook; do not join, work in continuous rnds—6 sc.

Place a marker in last sc made to indicate end of rnd. Move marker up as each rnd is completed.

Rnd 2: Work 2 sc in each st around—12 sc.

Rnd 3: [2 sc in next st, sc in next st] around—18 sc.

Rnd 4: [Sc in next st, 2 sc in next st, sc in next st] around—24 sc.

Rnd 5: [2 sc in next st, sc in next 3 sts] around—30 sc.

Rnd 6: [Sc in next 2 sts, 2 sc in next st, sc in next 2 sts] around—36 sc.

Rnd 7: [2 sc in next st, sc in next 5 sts] around—42 sc.

Rnds 8–10: Sc in each st around.

Rnd 11: Working in BLO, sc in each st around.

Rnd 12: [Inv-dec, sc in next 5 sts] around—36 sc.

Rnd 13: [Sc in next 2 sts, inv-dec, sc in next 2 sts] around—30 sc.

Rnd 14: [Inv-dec, sc in next 3 sts] around—24 sc.

Rnd 15: [Sc in next st, inv-dec, sc in next st] around—18 sc.

Fasten off.

Stalk

With B, beg at top of Stalk and, leaving a long beg tail for sewing, ch 2.

Rnd 1: Work 6 sc in 2nd ch from hook; do not join, work in continuous rnds—6 sc.

Place a marker in last sc made to indicate end of rnd. Move marker up as each rnd is completed.

Rnd 2: Work 2 sc in each st around—12 sc.

Rnd 3: [2 sc in next st, sc in next st] around—18 sc.

Rnd 4: Working in BLO, sc in each st around.

Rnd 5: [2 sc in next st, sc in next 5 sts] around—21 sc.

Rnds 6–8: Sc in each st around.

Rnd 9: [Sc in next 3 sts, 2 sc in next st, sc in next 3 sts] around—24 sc.

Rnds 10–12: Sc in each st around.

Add safety eyes between Rnds 7 and 8, about 3 sts apart.

Rnd 13: [2 sc in next st, sc in next 7 sts] around—27 sc.

Rnds 14–16: Sc in each st around.

Fasten off.

Stalk Bottom

With B, ch 2.

Rnd 1: Work 6 sc in 2nd ch from hook; do not join, work in continuous rnds—6 sc.

Place a marker in last sc made to indicate end of rnd. Move marker up as each rnd is completed.

Rnd 2: Work 2 sc in each st around—12 sc.

Rnd 3: [2 sc in next st, sc in next st] around—18 sc.

Rnd 4: [Sc in next st, 2 sc in next st, sc in next st] around—24 sc.

Rnd 5: [2 sc in next st, sc in next 7 sts] around—27 sc.

Fasten off, leaving a long tail for sewing.

Spots (Make as many as desired)

With C, ch 2.

Rnd 1: Work 6 sc in 2nd ch from hook; join with sl st in first sc—6 sc.

Fasten off, leaving a long tail for sewing.

Finishing

Sew Stalk Bottom to lower edge of Stalk.

Stuff Stalk and Cap.

Sew top of Stalk to bottom of Cap.

Sew Spot(s) to top of Cap. Cut additional spots from white felt and sew or glue to Cap.

Cut a piece of black craft wire about 2½ to 3 times as long as the width of the Stalk. Gently poke the wire through center of Stalk at arm level, leaving equal-length ends sticking out of sides for arms.

Using black embroidery thread, embroider a smile in a V shape below the eyes.

Write or print an inspirational message on card stock and cut to desired size. Use hot glue or double-sided tape to attach sign to hands.

Weave in ends.

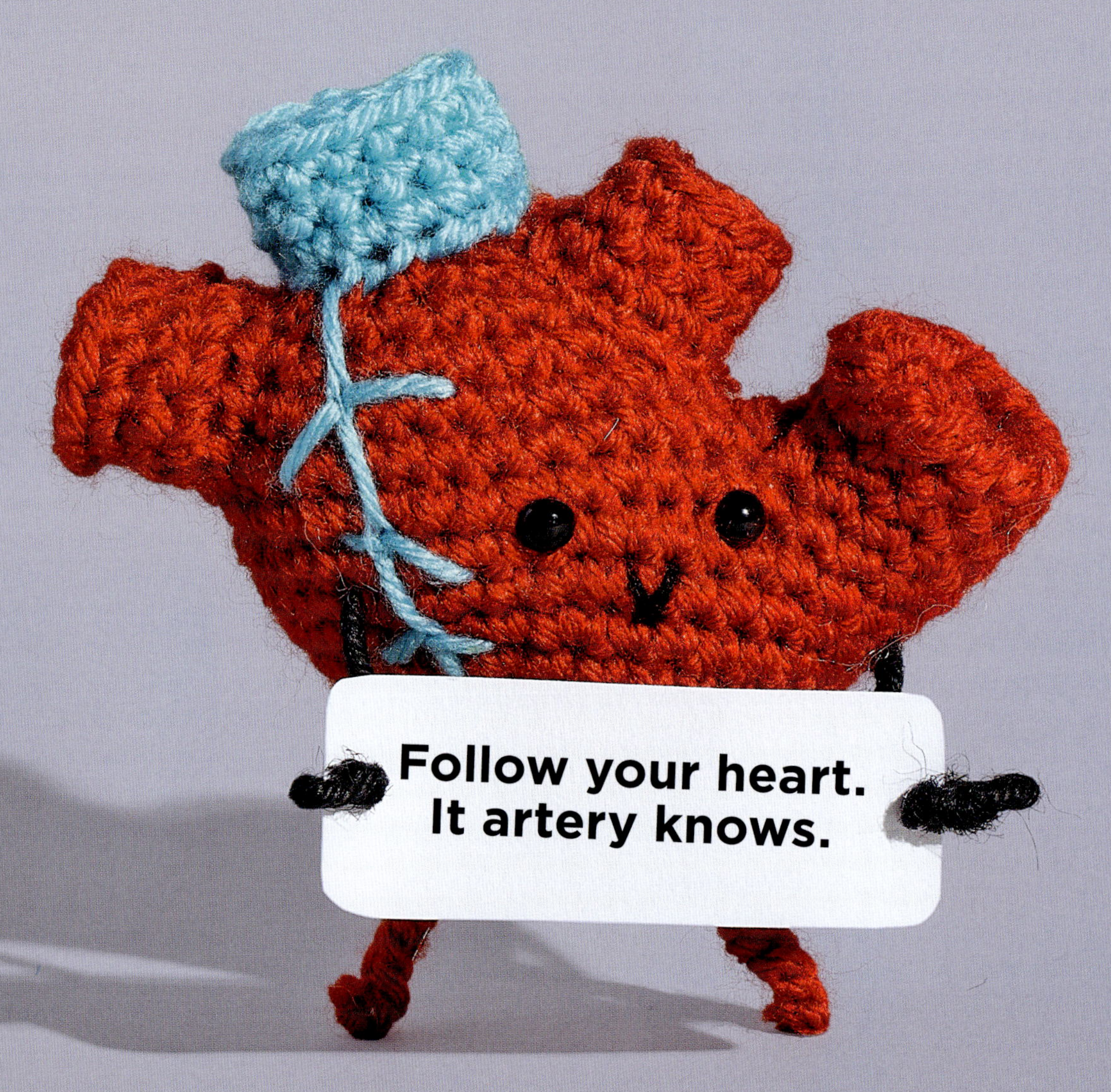
Follow your heart.
It artery knows.

HEART

Wow, look at you getting into such a good rhythm! You're keeping up with the pressure and getting things done! And now that you have some free time, you can go ahead and crochet this adorable heart without even skipping a beat!

AFFIRMATIONS for THE HEART

Follow your heart. It artery knows.

You make my heart skip a beat.

You're all heart.

You've got rhythm!

Don't let the pressure get to you.

Measurements
3½" (8.9 cm) × 4" (10.2 cm)

Yarn
Worsted weight (#4 medium)

Shown here: Lion Brand Vanna's Choice, 170 yd (156 m), 3½ oz (100 g), 100% acrylic: 1 ball 860-113 Scarlet (A)

WeCrochet Brava Worsted, 218 yd (200 m), 3½ oz (100 g), 100% acrylic: 1 ball 28422 Corn Flower (B)

Hook
US Size G/6 (4 mm) crochet hook. Adjust hook size if necessary to work tightly.

Gauge
Exact gauge is not critical for this piece. Work tightly to ensure stuffing does not show through.

Notions
Yarn needle
Polyester stuffing
Black embroidery thread
Black craft wire
1 pair 6 mm black safety eyes
Scissors
Stitch marker
Card stock
Hot glue or double-sided tape

Body

With A, ch 2.

Rnd 1: Work 6 sc in 2nd ch from hook; do not join, work in continuous rnds—6 sc.

Place marker in last sc made to indicate end of rnd. Move marker up as each rnd is completed.

Rnd 2: Work 2 sc in each st around—12 sc.

Rnd 3: [2 sc in next st, sc in next 3 sts] around—15 sc.

Rnd 4: [Sc in next 2 sts, 2 sc in next st, sc in next 2 sts] around—18 sc.

Rnd 5: [2 sc in next st, sc in next 5 sts] around—21 sc.

Rnd 6: [Sc in next 3 sts, 2 sc in next st, sc in next 3 sts] around—24 sc.

Rnd 7: [2 sc in next st, sc in next 7 sts] around—27 sc.

Rnd 8: [Sc in next 4 sts, 2 sc in next st, sc in next 4 sts] around—30 sc.

Rnd 9: [2 sc in next st, sc in next 9 sts] around—33 sc.

Rnd 10: [Sc in next 5 sts, 2 sc in next st, sc in next 5 sts] around—36 sc.

Rnd 11: [2 sc in next st, sc in next 11 sts] around—39 sc.

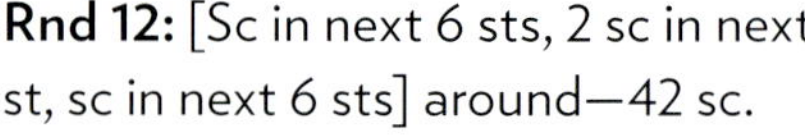

Rnd 12: [Sc in next 6 sts, 2 sc in next st, sc in next 6 sts] around—42 sc.

Rnd 13: Sk first 12 sts (artery opening made), sc in remaining 30 sts—30 sc.

Rnd 14: Sc in each st around—30 sc.

Rnd 15: [Inv-dec, sc in next 3 sts] around—24 sc.

Rnd 16: [Sc in next st, inv-dec, sc in next st] around—18 sc.

Rnd 17: [Inv-dec, sc in next st] around—12 sc.

Rnd 18: Inv-dec around—6 sc.

Fasten off, leaving a tail for sewing. Sew remaining 6 sts closed.

Working through opening made in Rnd 13, add safety eyes between Rnds 11 and 12, about 3 sts apart. Stuff Body, and continue stuffing as work progresses.

Artery

With A, join to any of the 12 skipped sts of Rnd 13 of Body.

Rnds 1–3: Sc in each st around; do not join, work in continuous rnds—12 sc.

Fasten off.

Artery Cap

With A, ch 2.

Rnd 1: Work 6 sc in 2nd ch from hook; do not join, work in continuous rnds—6 sc.

Rnd 2: Work 2 sc in each st around—12 sc.

Rnd 3: Sc in each st around.

Fasten off, leaving a long tail for sewing.

Valve (Make 3—2 with A, and 1 with B)

Leaving a long beg tail for sewing, ch 12; sl st in first ch to form a ring.

Rnd 1: Ch 1, sc in each ch around; do not join, work in continuous rnds—12 sc.

Rnds 2 and 3: Sc around.

Fasten off.

Legs (Make 1)

With A, ch 20.

Fasten off and trim ends.

Finishing

Stuff Artery. Sew Artery Cap to top of Artery.

Sew Valves to top of Body with blue Valve in the center.

With B and using photograph as a guide, embroider veins on front of Heart.

Cut a piece of black craft wire about 2½ to 3 times as long as the width of the piece. Gently poke the wire through center of piece at arm level, leaving equal-length ends sticking out of sides for arms.

Thread Legs through bottom of Body, leaving equal-length ends of ch-20 hanging down for legs. With a length of A, sew a few stitches to secure Legs.

Using black embroidery thread, embroider a smile in a V shape below the eyes.

Write or print an inspirational message on card stock and cut to desired size. Use hot glue or double-sided tape to attach sign to hands.

Weave in ends.

GHOST

This sweet little ghost is the perfect reminder that your spirit shines bright, even when you feel a little "invisible." With a playful smile and positive energy, this ghost encourages you to embrace your uniqueness and spread kindness—because your light will always be felt, even in the dark.

AFFIRMATIONS for THE GHOST

You have a boo-tiful spirit.

You're so good, it's spooky!

If you've got it, haunt it!

You're specter-cular!

You float through life with love and light.

Measurements
3" (7.6 cm) × 2½" (6.4 cm)

Yarn
Worsted weight (#4 medium)

Shown here: WeCrochet Brava Worsted 218 yd (200 m), 3½ oz (100 g), 100% acrylic: 1 ball 28455 White

Hook
US Size G/6 (4 mm) crochet hook. Adjust hook size if necessary to work tightly.

Gauge
Exact gauge is not critical for this piece. Work tightly to ensure stuffing does not show through.

Notions
Yarn needle
Polyester stuffing
Black embroidery thread
Black craft wire
1 pair 6 mm black safety eyes
Sparkle pink felt
Scissors
Stitch marker
Card stock
Hot glue or double-sided tape

You have
a boo-tiful
spirit.

Body

Ch 2.

Rnd 1: Work 6 sc in 2nd ch from hook; do not join, work in continuous rnds—6 sc.

Place a marker in last sc made to indicate end of rnd. Move marker up as each rnd is completed.

Rnd 2: Work 2 sc in each st around—12 sc.

Rnd 3: [2 sc in next st, sc in next st] around—18 sc.

Rnd 4: [Sc in next st, 2 sc in next, sc in next st] around—24 sc.

Rnd 5: [2 sc in next st, sc in next 3 sts] around—30 sc.

Rnd 6: [Sc in next 2 sts, 2 sc in next st, sc in next 2 sts] around—36 sc.

Rnds 7–16: Sc in each st around.

Fasten off. Add circles of pink felt to back of safety eyes and trim using photo as a guide. Add eyes between Rnds 9 and 10, about 3 sts apart.

Bottom

Ch 2.

Rnds 1–6: Work same as Rnds 1–6 of Body—36 sc.

Fasten off, leaving a long tail for sewing.

Finishing

Stuff Body.

Cut a piece of black craft wire about 2½ to 3 times as long as the width of the Body. Gently poke the wire through center of Body at arm level, leaving equal-length ends sticking out of sides for arms.

Using black embroidery thread, embroider a smile in a V shape below the eyes.

Sew Bottom to lower edge of Body, sewing through BLO of Body sts, and FLO of Bottom sts to leave an edge.

Trim

Join yarn to any edge stitch along bottom of Body.

Rnd 1: Ch 1, beg in same st as join, [sc in next st, sk next 2 sts, 5 dc in next st, sk next 2 sts] around; join with sl st in first sc—36 sts (six 5-dc groups and 6 sc).

Fasten off.

Write or print an inspirational message on card stock and cut to desired size. Use hot glue or double-sided tape to attach sign to hands.

Weave in ends.

HOUSE PLANT

Aloe, gorgeous! You are incredible, remarkable, truly un-be-leaf-able! No matter what today has in store, you can carry this little plant with you and remind yourself that we're all rooting for you!

AFFIRMATIONS for THE HOUSE PLANT

Be-leaf in yourself.

Plant one on me.

Grow positive thoughts!

You're un-be-leaf-able.

I'm rooting for you.

Measurements
3½" (8.9 cm) × 2½" (6.4 cm)

Yarn
Worsted weight (#4 medium)

Shown here: Lion Brand Basic Stitch Anti Pilling, 185 yd (170 m), 3½ oz (100 g), 100% acrylic: 1 ball each 202-112S Deco Rose (A) and 202-125AA Truffle (B)

Lion Brand Vanna's Choice, 170 yd (156 m), 3½ oz (100 g), 100% acrylic: 1 ball 860-172C Kelly Green (C)

Hook
US Size G/6 (4 mm) crochet hook. Adjust hook size if necessary to work tightly.

Gauge
Exact gauge is not critical for this piece. Work tightly to ensure stuffing does not show through.

Notions
Yarn needle
Polyester stuffing
Black embroidery thread
Black craft wire
1 pair 6 mm black safety eyes
Scissors
Stitch marker
Card stock
Hot glue or double-sided tape

Be-leaf in yourself.

Pot

With A, make a magic loop.

Rnd 1: Work 6 sc in loop; do not join. Work in continuous rnds—6 sc.

Place marker in last sc made to indicate end of rnd. Move marker up as each rnd is completed.

Rnd 2: Work 2 sc in each st around—12 sc.

Rnd 3: [2 sc in next st, sc in next st] around—18 sc.

Rnd 4: [Sc in next st, 2 sc in next st, sc in next st] around—24 sc.

Rnd 5: [2 sc in next st, sc in next 3 sts] around—30 sc.

Rnds 6 and 7: Working in BLO, sl st in each st around—30 sl sts.

Rnd 8: Working in BLO, sc in each st around.

Rnds 9 and 10: Sc in each st around.

Rnd 11: [2 sc in next st, sc in next 9 sts] around—33 sc.

Rnd 12: Sc in each st around.

Rnd 13: [Sc in next 5 sts, 2 sc in next st, sc in next 5 sts] around—36 sc.

Rnd 14: Sc in each st around.

Rnd 15: Working in BLO, sc in each st around.

Rnd 16: Hdc in each free FLO of Rnd 14—36 hdc.

Rnd 17: Working in BLO, sl st in each st around—36 sl sts.

Fasten off. Add safety eyes between Rnds 10 and 11, about 4 sts apart.

Stuff Pot.

Soil

With B, make a magic loop.

Rnds 1–5: Work same as Rnds 1–5 of Pot—30 sc.

Rnd 6: [Sc in next 2 sts, 2 sc in next st, sc in next 2 sts] around—36 sc.

Fasten off, leaving a long tail for sewing.

Leaves (Make 4)

With C, ch 3.

Row 1: (Sc, hdc, sc) in 2nd ch from hook (leaf made), sl st in next ch, [ch 5, (sc, hdc, sc) in 2nd ch from hook (leaf made), sl st in next ch, sk last 2 ch] 3 times; rotate piece to work along opposite side of chains (to work last 3 leaves), [sl st across to base of next leaf, ch 3, (sc, hdc, sc) in 2nd ch from hook, sl st in next ch] 3 times—7 Leaves.

Fasten off, leaving a long tail for sewing.

Finishing

Sew Soil to top of Pot.

Sew each set of Leaves to top of Soil.

Cut a piece of black craft wire about 2½ to 3 times as long as the width of the piece. Gently poke the wire through center of Pot at arm level, leaving equal-length ends sticking out of sides for arms.

Using black embroidery thread, embroider a smile in a V shape below the eyes.

Write or print an inspirational message on card stock and cut to desired size. Use hot glue or double-sided tape to attach sign to hands.

Weave in ends.

TRAFFIC CONE

Setting boundaries can be difficult, but it's necessary sometimes. Take this traffic cone with you throughout your day and when life gets tough, just remember to stay cone-fident!

AFFIRMATIONS for THE TRAFFIC CONE

Know your boundaries.

You stop traffic.

Stay alert!

Proceed with caution.

Be cone-fident!

Measurements
3½" (8.9 cm) × 3" (7.6 cm)

Yarn
Worsted weight (#4 medium)

Shown here: Lion Brand Basic Stitch Anti Pilling, 185 yd (170 m), 3½ oz (100 g), 100% acrylic: 1 ball each 202-133A Pumpkin (A) and 202-100 White (B).

Hook
US Size G/6 (4 mm) crochet hook. Adjust hook size if necessary to work tightly.

Gauge
Exact gauge is not critical for this piece. Work tightly to ensure stuffing does not show through.

Notions
Yarn needle
Polyester stuffing
Black embroidery thread
Black craft wire
1 pair 6 mm black safety eyes
Scissors
Stitch marker
Card stock
Hot glue or double-sided tape

Know your
boundaries.

Cone

With A, ch 2.

Rnd 1: Work 4 sc in 2nd ch from hook; join with sl st in first sc—4 sc.

Rnd 2: Ch 1, [2 sc in next st, sc in next st] around; join with sl st in first sc—6 sc.

Rnd 3: Ch 1, working in BLO, [sc in next st, 2 sc in next st, sc in next st] around; join with sl st in first sc—8 sc.

Rnd 4: Ch 1, [2 sc in next st, sc in next 3 sts] around; join with sl st in first sc—10 sc.

Rnd 5: Ch 1, [sc in next 2 sts, 2 sc in next st, sc in next 2 sts] around; join with sl st in first sc—12 sc.

Rnd 6: Ch 1, [2 sc in next st, sc in next 5 sts] around; join with sl st in first sc—14 sc.

Rnd 7: Ch 1, [sc in next 3 sts, 2 sc in next st, sc in next 3 sts] around; join with sl st in first sc—16 sc.

Rnd 8: Ch 1, [2 sc in next st, sc in next 7 sts] around; join with sl st in first sc—18 sc.

Change to B.

Rnd 9: Ch 1, working in BLO, [sc in next 4 sts, 2 sc in next st, sc in next 4 sts] around; join with sl st in first sc—20 sc.

Rnd 10: Ch 1, [2 sc in next st, sc in next 9 sts] around; join with sl st in first sc—22 sc.

Change to A.

Rnd 11: Ch 1, working in BLO, [sc in next 5 sts, 2 sc in next st, sc in next 5 sts] around; join with sl st in first sc—24 sc.

Rnd 12: Ch 1, [2 sc in next st, sc in next 11 sts] around; join with sl st in first sc—26 sc.

Rnd 13: Ch 1, [sc in next 6 sts, 2 sc in next st, sc in next 6 sts] around; join with sl st in first sc—28 sc.

Rnd 14: Ch 1, [2 sc in next st, sc in next 13 sts] around; join with sl st in first sc—30 sc.

Change to B.

Rnd 15: Ch 1, working in BLO, [sc in next 7 sts, 2 sc in next st, sc in next 7 sts] around; join with sl st in first sc—32 sc.

Rnd 16: Ch 1, [2 sc in next st, sc in next 15 sts] around; join with sl st in first sc—34 sc.

Change to A.

Rnd 17: Ch 1, working in BLO, [sc in next 8 sts, 2 sc in next st, sc in next

8 sts] around; join with sl st in first sc—36 sc.

Rnd 18: Ch 1, [2 sc in next st, sc in next 17 sts] around; join with sl st in first sc—38 sc.

Rnd 19: Ch 1, [sc in next 9 sts, 2 sc in next st, sc in next 9 sts] around; join with sl st in first sc—40 sc.

Rnd 20: Ch 1, [2 sc in next st, sc in next 19 sts] around; join with sl st in first sc—42 sc.

Rnd 21: Ch 1, working in FLO, sc in each st around; join with sl st in first sc.

Fasten off, leaving a long tail for sewing. Add safety eyes between Rnds 13 and 14, about 4 sts apart.

Stuff Cone.

Bottom (Make 2)

With A, ch 15.

Row 1: Sc in 2nd ch from hook and in each ch across, turn—14 sc.

Rows 2–15: Ch 1, sc across, turn. Do not turn at the end of Row 15.

Fasten off first piece, do not fasten off 2nd piece.

Rnd 16 (joining): Hold Bottom pieces together with stitches matching, ch 1, working through both thicknesses, work 15 sc evenly spaced in ends of rows along side edge, ch 1; working along opposite side of foundation ch, 2 sc in first ch, sc in next 13 ch, ch 1; work 15 sc evenly spaced in ends of rows along next side edge, ch 1, 2 sc in first st of Row 15, sc in each st across, ch 1; join with sl st in first sc—60 sc and 4 ch-1 corner sps.

Fasten off.

Finishing

Sew Cone to Bottom.

Cut a piece of black craft wire about 2½ to 3 times as long as the width of the piece. Gently poke the wire through center of Cone at arm level, leaving equal-length ends sticking out of sides for arms.

Using black embroidery thread, embroider a smile in a V shape below the eyes.

Write or print an inspirational message on card stock and cut to desired size. Use hot glue or double-sided tape to attach sign to hands.

Weave in ends.

Don't forget hue you are.

GRAYONS

Hey there, colorful soul! We love to see your colors shine bright! But even if you have the blues, don't forget that even broken crayons still color! Enjoy crocheting these adorable crayon amigurumi in any color you choose! The possibilities for color-specific affirmations are endless.

AFFIRMATIONS for THE CRAYON

Don't forget hue you are.

You're the brightest crayon in the box!

You color the world with awesomeness.

Don't be afraid to color outside the lines.

Let your colors shine bright.

Measurements
6½" (16.5 cm) × 1½" (3.8 cm)

Yarn
Worsted weight (#4 medium)

Shown here:
Red Crayon: WeCrochet Swish Worsted 110 yd (100 m), 1¾ oz (50 g), 100% fine superwash merino wool: 1 ball each N4131 Phoenix (A) and 23876 Black (C)

Lion Brand Vanna's Choice, 170 yd (156 m), 3½ oz (100 g), 100% acrylic: 1 ball 860-113 Scarlet (B)

Blue Crayon: WeCrochet Swish Worsted 110 yd (100 m), 1¾ oz (50 g), 100% fine superwash merino wool: 1 ball each 26645 Electric Blue (A), 28656 Arctic (B), and 23876 Black (C)

Purple Crayon: WeCrochet Swish Worsted 110 yd (100 m), 1¾ oz (50 g), 100% fine superwash merino wool: 1 ball each 25147 Amethyst Heather (A), N4108 Allium (B), and 23876 Black (C)

Hook
US Size G/6 (4 mm) crochet hook. Adjust hook size if necessary to work tightly.

Gauge
Exact gauge is not critical for this piece. Work tightly to ensure stuffing does not show through.

Notions
Yarn needle
Polyester stuffing
Black embroidery thread
Black craft wire
3 pairs of 6 mm black safety eyes
Scissors
Stitch marker
Card stock
Hot glue or double-sided tape

Crayon

With A, make a magic loop.

Rnd 1: Work 4 sc in loop; join with sl st in first sc—4 sc.

Rnd 2: Working in BLO, ch 1, sc in next 4 sc, sc in sl st used to join previous rnd, do not join—5 sc.

Rnd 3: Work 2 sc in next st, sc in each st around—6 sc.

Rnds 4–9: Rep Rnd 3—12 sc in Rnd 9.

Rnd 10: Work 2 sc in each st around—24 sc.

Rnd 11: Working in BLO, sc in each st around; join with sl st in first sc.

Change to B.

Rnd 12: Ch 1, sl st in each st around; join with sl st in first sl st—24 sl sts.

Rnd 13: Ch 1, working in BLO, sc in each st around; join with sl st in first sc.

Rnd 14: Ch 1, sc in each st around; join with sl st in first sc.

Change to C.

Rnds 15 and 16: Rep Rnds 12 and 13.

Change to B.

Rnd 17 and 18: Rep Rnds 12 and 13.

Change to C.

Rnds 19 and 20: Rep Rnds 12 and 13.

Change to B.

Rnds 21 and 22: Rep Rnds 12 and 13.

Rnd 23: Ch 1, sc in each st around, do not join.

Rnds 24–33: Sc in each st around, joining at the end of Rnd 33 only.

Add safety eyes between Rnds 29 and 30, about 3 sts apart.

Stuff Crayon and continue stuffing as work progresses.

Change to C.

Rnds 34–42: Rep Rnds 15–23, joining at the end of Rnd 42.

Change to A.

Rnds 43 and 44: Rep Rnds 12 and 13.

Rnd 45: Ch 1, working in BLO, [sc in next st, sc2tog, sc in next st] around; join with sl st in first sc—18 sc.

Rnd 46: Ch 1, [inv-dec, sc in next st] around; join with sl st in first st—12 sc.

Rnd 47: Ch 1, inv-dec around; join with sl st in first st—6 sc.

Fasten off, leaving a long tail for sewing. Sew remaining 6 sts closed.

Finishing

For each Crayon, cut a piece of black craft wire about 4 to 5 times as long as the width of the piece. Gently poke the wire through center of piece at arm level, leaving equal-length ends sticking out of sides for arms.

Using black embroidery thread, embroider smiles in a V shape below the eyes.

Write or print an inspirational message on card stock and cut to desired size. Use hot glue or double-sided tape to attach sign to hands.

Weave in ends.

ACORN

We all have to start somewhere, and even if your first step is tiny, it's important to cherish what you've accomplished and watch it grow into something big. Just like a little acorn that grows into a mighty oak tree, your actions today will have a big impact tomorrow! This little acorn believes you can with all her might!

AFFIRMATIONS for THE ACORN

Small but mighty

You're growing into something amazing.

From tiny acorns grow mighty oaks.

I'm nuts about you.

I may be small, but I'm packed with energy and ready to roll!

Measurements
3½" (8.9 cm) × 2" (5.1 cm)

Yarn
Worsted weight (#4 medium)

Shown here: Loops & Threads Impeccable, 277 yd (253 m), 4.5 oz (127.5 g), 100% acrylic: 1 ball 75 Heather (A)

Lion Brand Basic Stitch Anti Pilling,185 yd (170 m), 3½ oz (100 g), 100% acrylic: 1 ball 202-126AL Mahogany (B)

Hook
US Size G/6 (4 mm) crochet hook. Adjust hook size if necessary to work tightly.

Gauge
Exact gauge is not critical for this piece. Work tightly to ensure stuffing does not show through.

Notions
Yarn needle
Polyester stuffing
Black embroidery thread
Black craft wire
1 pair 6 mm black safety eyes
Pink blush
Scissors
Stitch marker
Card stock
Hot glue or double-sided tape

Small but mighty

Nut

With A, beg at bottom of piece, ch 2.

Rnd 1: Work 3 sc in 2nd ch from hook; do not join. Work in continuous rnds—3 sc.

Place marker in last sc made to indicate end of rnd. Move marker up as each rnd is completed.

Rnd 2: Work 2 sc in next st, sc in next 2 sts—4 sc.

Rnd 3: [2 sc in next st, sc in next st] around—6 sc.

Rnd 4: Work 2 sc in each st around—12 sc.

Rnd 5: [2 sc in next st, sc in next 3 sts] around—15 sc.

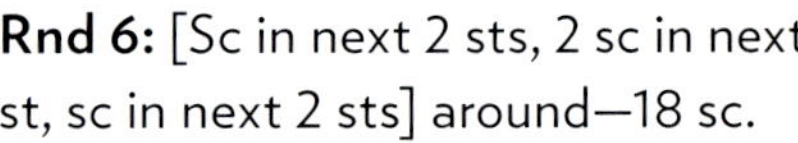

Rnd 6: [Sc in next 2 sts, 2 sc in next st, sc in next 2 sts] around—18 sc.

Rnd 7: [2 sc in next st, sc in next 5 sts] around—21 sc.

Rnd 8: [Sc in next 3 sts, 2 sc in next st, sc in next 3 sts] around—24 sc.

Rnd 9: [2 sc in next st, sc in next 7 sts] around—27 sc.

Rnd 10: [Sc in next 4 sts, 2 sc in next st, sc in next 4 sts] around—30 sc.

Rnds 11–14: Sc in each st around.

Add safety eyes between Rnds 10 and 11, about 5 sts apart. Stuff piece and continue stuffing as work progresses.

Rnd 15: [Inv-dec, sc in next 3 sts] around—24 sc.

Rnd 16: [Sc in next st, inv-dec, sc in next st] around—18 sc.

Rnd 17: [Inv-dec, sc in next st] around—12 sc.

Rnd 18: Inv-dec around—6 sc.

Fasten off, leaving a long tail for sewing. Sew remaining 6 sts closed.

Top

With B, ch 6.

Rnd 1: Sc in 2nd ch from hook, sc in next 3 ch (stem made), sc in next ch, place a marker in sc just made to indicate beg of rnd, work 5 more sc in marked ch; do not join, work in continuous rnds—10 sc.

Move marker up as each rnd is worked.

Rnd 2: Skip stem, work 2 sc in marked st, 2 sc in each of next 5 sts; leave stem unworked—12 sc.

Rnd 3: [2 sc in next st, sc in next st] around—18 sc.

Rnd 4: [Sc in next st, 2 sc in next st, sc in next st] around—24 sc.

Rnd 5: [2 sc in next st, sc in next 3 sts] around—30 sc.

Rnds 6 and 7: Sc in each st around.

Rnd 8: Working in BLO, sl st in each st around.

Fasten off, leaving a long tail for sewing.

Finishing

Sew Top to top of Nut.

Cut a piece of black craft wire about 2½ to 3 times as long as the width of the piece. Gently poke the wire through center of Nut at arm level, leaving equal-length ends sticking out of sides for arms.

Using black embroidery thread, embroider a smile in a V shape below the eyes.

Add a small amount of blush under each eye.

Write or print an inspirational message on card stock and cut to desired size. Use hot glue or double-sided tape to attach sign to hands.

Weave in ends.

Keep chasing
that pot of gold.

RAINBOW

When it rains, it pours. But even after a big storm there is always the chance of spotting a beautiful rainbow! Crochet this little cutie with big, fluffy clouds for a friend who needs a reminder that you think their friendship is the pot of gold at the end of the rainbow.

AFFIRMATIONS for THE RAINBOW

Keep chasing that pot of gold.

You're the rainbow after a storm.

Dreams really do come true.

When life gets stormy, remember the rainbow is just around the corner.

Measurements
3" (7.6 cm) × 4½" (11.4 cm)

Yarn
Worsted weight (#4 medium)

Shown here: Lion Brand Basic Stitch Anti Pilling, 185 yd (170 m), 3½ oz (100 g), 100% acrylic: 1 ball each 202-106A Baby Blue (A), 202-130B Grass (B), 202-158I Mustard (C), 202-133A Pumpkin (D), and 202-100 White (F)

Lion Brand Vanna's Choice, 170 yd (156 m), 3½ oz (100 g), 100% acrylic: 1 ball 860-113 Scarlet (E)

Hook
US Size G/6 (4 mm) crochet hook. Adjust hook size if necessary to work tightly.

Gauge
Exact gauge is not critical for this piece. Work tightly to ensure stuffing does not show through.

Notions
Yarn needle
Polyester stuffing
Black embroidery thread
Black craft wire
1 pair 6 mm black safety eyes
Scissors
Stitch marker
Card stock
Hot glue or double-sided tape

Rainbow (Make 2)

With A, leaving a long beg tail for sewing, ch 7.

Row 1: Sc in 2nd ch from hook, sc in next 5 ch, turn—6 sc.

Row 2: Ch 1, [2 sc in next st, sc in next st] across, turn—9 sc.

Change to B.

Row 3: Ch 1, [2 sc in next st, sc in next 2 sts] across, turn—12 sc.

Row 4: Ch 1, [2 sc in next st, sc in next 3 sts] across, turn—15 sc.

Change to C.

Row 5: Ch 1, [2 sc in next st, sc in next 4 sts] across, turn—18 sc.

Row 6: Ch 1, [2 sc in next st, sc in next 5 sts] across, turn—21 sc.

Change to D.

Row 7: Ch 1, [2 sc in next st, sc in next 6 sts] across, turn—24 sc.

Row 8: Ch 1, [2 sc in next st, sc in next 7 sts] across, turn—27 sc.

Change to E.

Row 9: Ch 1, [2 sc in next st, sc in next 8 sts] across, turn—30 sc.

Row 10: Ch 1, [2 sc in next st, sc in next 9 sts] across, turn—33 sc.

Fasten off, leaving a long tail for sewing.

Cloud Cap (Make 2)

With F, make a magic loop.

Rnd 1: Work 6 sc in loop; do not join. Work in continuous rnds—6 sc.

Place marker in last sc made to indicate end of rnd. Move marker up as each rnd is completed.

Rnd 2: Work 2 sc in each st around—12 sc.

Rnd 3: [2 sc in next st, sc in next st] around—18 sc.

Rnd 4: [Sc in next st, 2 sc in next st, sc in next st] around—24 sc.

Fasten off, leaving a long tail for sewing.

Cloud (Make 2)

With F, make a magic loop.

Rnds 1–4: Work same as Rnds 1–4 of Cloud Cap—24 sc.

Rnd 5: [2 sc in next st, sc in next 3 sts] around—30 sc.

Rnds 6–8: Sc in each st around.

Rnd 9: [Inv-dec, sc in next 3 sts] around—24 sc.

Rnd 10: [Sc in next st, inv-dec, sc in next st] around—18 sc.

Rnd 11: [Inv-dec, sc in next st] around—12 sc.

Stuff Cloud.

Rnd 12: Inv-dec around—6 sc.

Fasten off, leaving a long tail for sewing. Thread tail onto needle and insert needle inside Cloud and out through center of top. Wrap tail down side of Cloud and back into bottom of piece, pulling tight to cinch fabric. Repeat and cinch the opposite side of Cloud. Create 2 more cinches between first two cinches, dividing shape into 4 cinched sections.

Finishing

Sew last rows of Body pieces together to create top seam. Sew first rows of Body pieces together to create bottom seam. Add safety eyes between Rows 3 and 4 of front of Rainbow, about 2 sts apart. Using black embroidery thread, embroider a smile in a V shape below the eyes.

Stuff Rainbow.

Sew a Cloud Cap to the bottom of each end of Rainbow.

Using a length of F, sew a Cloud to bottom of each Cloud Cap.

Cut a piece of black craft wire about 2½ to 3 times as long as the width of the piece. Gently poke the wire through piece near top of Rainbow, leaving equal-length ends sticking out of sides for arms.

Write or print an inspirational message on card stock and cut to desired size. Use hot glue or double-sided tape to attach sign to hands.

Weave in ends.

ABOUT THE AUTHOR

Lee Sartori is the crochet designer behind CoCo Crochet Lee. Lee's passion is designing modern, wearable garments, and adorable amigurumi. The author of six previous crochet books, she was formerly a guest host on the popular PBS/CreateTV Show *Knit and Crochet Now*, as well as a cast member of Annie's Creative Studio. Lee lives in Halifax, Canada, with her two children, her amazing husband, her adorable bunny, Neville, and two cats, Ginny and Toast.

Keep on cluckin'!	You're the cat's meow.	You are dino-mite!	You're owl that.	Take your time!	Best Friend
Stay sharp!	It's okay to take up space.	You have a boo-tiful spirit.	Be-leaf in yourself.	Know your boundaries.	Don't forget hue you are.
Small but mighty	You're kind of a big dill.	Donut give up!	Positive Potato	You've guac this!	I relish spending time with you!
Keep on the sunny side.	Nothing is im-popsicle!	You're one cool chick.	I dino what I'd do without you.	Keep calm and carry on.	You are wise beyond measure.
Don't let anyone dull your flame.	Hang in there!	Feline good!	You're always on point.	You're out of this world!	I love you very mush.
If you've got it, haunt it!	I'm rooting for you.	Proceed with caution.	Positive Pickle	I'll never dessert you.	Let's guac and roll.
You've got the recipe for success.	Live with a-bun-dance.	Chill out, you're crushing it!	You make my heart skip a beat.	Don't get your feathers ruffled.	You've got cat-titude.
You're pterrific!	Slow and steady wins the race.	I'm owl-ways here for you.	You're juggling a lot.	If you're dragon, I'll be there to pick you up.	Slow down and enjoy the journey.
You're top dog.	Be the mane character of your story.	You thrive no matter the conditions.	You run rings around the competition.	Need some morel support?	Don't let the pressure get to you.
You're specter-cular!	Grow positive thoughts!	You stop traffic.	You're the brightest crayon in the box!	I'm nuts about you.	You're the rainbow after a storm.
Keep gherkin it!	Enjoy the sweet side of life!	I'll be frank. You're the best.	You're my best spud.	Let's avo-cuddle.	You're on a roll!

Cut along dotted lines.

You're making progress at your own pace.

Optimistic Octopus

You're the stuff of legends.

I ain't lion, you're the best!

I have so mushroom in my heart for you.

Follow your heart. It artery knows.

Keep chasing that pot of gold.

Wow, look at you! Taco-bout incredible!

You're one smart cookie!

You're the pine-apple of my eye.

I'm not kitten around, you're the best!

There's nothing you can't hand-le.

Life would be "ruff" without you!

You're tough on the outside, but sweet on the inside.

Don't be afraid to color outside the lines.

When life gets stormy, remember the rainbow is just around the corner.

From tiny acorns grow mighty oaks.

A taco is spicy and full of zest—just like you!

I may be just a tiny potato, but I believe in you!

Egg-cellent things are coming your way.

Life's a fiesta—celebrate every bite!

Cut along dotted lines.